A Woman Standing

Carmen Stenholm, Ph.D.

Dragon's Egg Press

What People Are Saying ...

In her first offering, CRACK BETWEEN THE WORLDS Carmen Stenholm vividly brought to life four generations of her family's stories. In A WOMAN STANDING, she boldly and candidly delves more deeply into her story, a complex weave of tragedy and triumph. The work becomes compelling when the reader discovers they only have to insert their name into the narrative and her journey becomes their story too. They, like Carmen, have had tragedy, unspeakable hurt, unending pain and, as with Carmen, they can chose, either to let the pain overwhelm them or define them to triumph.

A WOMAN STANDING will speak to your soul and reminds us that everyone has hurt in their lives. It is what we chose to do with that hurt that will either leave us standing or defeated.

Paul Bruno, PgMP, PMP, author of *Project Management in History: The First Jeep*

A WOMAN STANDING is a beautiful and insightful story that highlights the internal struggle and ultimate triumph over life challenges and tragedies. The authentic vignettes strike a chord in the reader that they can relate to with both empathy and compassion. My experience reading these words was moving and emotional. I enjoyed the strength that Karin displayed by overcoming those things that were out of her control. I am left with the sense of connection and celebration for all women! Thank you, Carmen.

Becky Cox, artist, art educator, art therapist, AHA Artful Healing Academy

Carmen Stenholm's novel is a quick, impactful read -- especially for those of us who have struggled to create new life out of the chaos and pain World War II inflicted on our parents. When Karin and her mother escape East Germany and immigrate to the United States, starting over at age ten wasn't as easy as she had anticipated. Sensitive, shy, and trusting, she is further traumatized by childhood rejections, sexual abuse and her mother's emotional instability. She marries young and has a small child when her husband abandons her. The arc of Karin's journey to independence, security, and love plays out on the tenderly-written pages of this book.

I recommend this book for cool, rainy days ... made more delicious by snuggling between crisp sheets and warm quilts. Karin's struggles are unique yet boomers will surely recognize elements their own angst-ridden young adulthood in her tale.

Joyce Faulkner, author of *Vala's Bed, Windshift,* and *In the Shadow of Suribachi*

"We lumber and lurch until we become all of the light we can see. A WOMAN STANDING allows us to be a witness and a presence to this marvelous process." My heartfelt desire is that those who will read the book will, through your words, find the hope and fortitude to move forward in joy.

Genevieve L. McDowell, faculty of Cal Poly University in Pomona, California in music/voice (ret)

After reading Carmen Stenholm's book, CRACK BETWEEN THE WORLDS, I was anxious to read her sequel to see the ongoing journey of strong women in East Germany and America. Her second book, A WOMAN STANDING, does not disappoint. It extends the strength and tenacity of the generations of these women into the present. Courage, persistence and the ability to not only overcome, but succeed in life is very palpable in this book. This book gives honor to her family line and hope to all who read it.

This is a profound read. It reveals a generational courage and strength to cross boarders, walk through adversity and stand tall. Thank you Dr. Stenholm!

Laura Knowles, RN, hospital administrator and educator

Like amulets on a charm bracelet or a series of snapshots in a newly-discovered photo album, A WOMAN STANDING deftly weaves single scraps of story fabric into an intimate and satisfying patchwork quilt of a life.

Eschewing rigidly defined timelines and descriptions one chapter happens a month after its predecessor; the next occurs ten years later Carmen Stenholm creates a diary of the heart. Each short chapter leaves the reader with a strong feeling, a deep insight and a thirst to delve into the next one.

Connie Donaldson, author of *Dumping The Magic*

"The lifetime effects of war, abuse, and loneliness are hard to imagine in any given timeline. However, Stenholm creates a vision of time and place for her readers and, even more importantly, shows how lives in apparent ruin, can survive on hope. Much more than a good read, it is inspirational".

Kathy Cieslewicz, artist and curator of the Sears Art Museum Gallery at Dixie State University, St George, UT

A WOMAN STANDING is a testimonial to who we choose to be. A life long journey of empathy and self-preservation.

A story whose roots we first experience in CRACK BETWEEN THE WORLDS that reminds us that life is a process in which patience is key and that there are no crystal balls.

One comes away from A WOMAN STANDING enlightened, refreshed, and amazed.

Gayle Eisenberg, B.A. In English, careers in Contracts Administration and in Optical Sales

Copyright 2017   Carmen Stenholm

All Rights Reserved. No part of this book shall be reproduced or transmitted in any form or by any means, electronic, mechanical, magnetic, photographic including photocopying, recording or by any information storage and retrieval system, without prior written permission of the author.

ISBN: 978-0-692-93453-1   Soft cover

LCCN: 2017914344

Art by: Christina G. Bourne

Dragon's Egg Press

Saint George, UT

Printed in the USA

Dedication

For my husband, Karl, who brought me from the brink of resignation to renewed wonder and joy.

*Backstory is told in CRACK BETWEEN THE WORLDS

Acknowledgements

Karl, my husband, who believed in me and supported this work from its beginning to its end, has my everlasting gratitude.

No major undertaking is possible without the love and support of a host of friends and colleagues. It is my great fortune to have innumerable people in my life who gave selflessly of their time and talents to support this effort.

There are also many people who, without ever having met me, spent their time and energy to read this manuscript. It will never be possible to put into words how grateful I am for your generosity.

Last, but decidedly not least, I am grateful to you, the reader. I hope you will find a part of your own story in this one.

CONTENTS

Part I 3
Saying Goodbye 3
Chapter 1 1
Chapter 2 9

Part II 13
New Beginnings 13
Chapter 3 15
Chapter 4 17
Chapter 5 19

Part III 23
Too Young to be Old 23
Chapter 6 25
Chapter 7 31

Part IV 35
Love? 35
Chapter 8 37
Chapter 9 41
Chapter 10 43

Part V 47
Moving Forward 47
Chapter 11 49

Chapter 12	51
Chapter 13	55
Chapter 14	57
Part VI	**63**
More New Beginnings	63
Chapter 15	65
Chapter 16	69
Chapter 17	71
Chapter 18	75
Part VII	**81**
Moving On	81
Chapter 19	83
Chapter 20	87
Chapter 21	93
Chapter 22	97
Chapter 23	101
Chapter 24	105
Chapter 25	109
Note to Reader	115

Part I

Saying Goodbye

Chapter 1

For the first ten years of my life, I knew who I was. That was one short decade before I became a daughter of the enemy.

Herbert, my father, was a Luftwaffe pilot who fought for his country until Germany was defeated in 1945. Like so many other young men of his generation, he came home not only defeated in battle but defeated in spirit. He brought home a young Norwegian wife and their tiny son. The son was welcome. His mother, Ilse, was not.

"Ich nehme meinen Sohn und gehe nach hause (I am taking my son and going home)," she shouted one fed-up day. "Your mother has turned her back on me and our neighbors ignore me. There is no one here who wants me, least of all the trollop you spend so much time with." A few months later, after her divorce from my father was final, Ilse took her son and returned to Norway.

Not long after that, my mother Ella, the "trollop," became pregnant. She gave birth to me in March of the next year, an ordeal for which she never really forgave me. A year and a half later, they married: the nineteen-year-old woman and the handsome pilot, thirteen years her senior. I was almost two years old and a flower girl when they married. Next to me was my neighbor, Werner, only a year older than I was. We were both dressed in white and proudly walked down the aisle of the courthouse pulling white rose petals out of our white baskets. My parents followed arm in arm. Ella was beautiful in her white lace gown with a long veil stirred by a breeze drifting through the tall courthouse doors. They were gorgeous, these two. No one was pleased.

My parents came home from their weeklong honeymoon in Ueckermuende and we moved from a loft into a two-bedroom apartment on the first floor of our building. It took almost no time for the arguments to begin. "Du verdammtes Luder (You goddamned bitch)!" Dad was yelling again and mother was sobbing and screaming incoherently. They were in the bedroom across the old hall but it sounded like they were in the kitchen with Oma and me. Oma was scrubbing my back while I sat in the tin bathtub we hauled up from the cellar once a month. Between large wooden crates, the tin tub usually leaned against the oldest wall in our building. Over four hundred years old, it had housed generation after generation of residents, mostly workers in the old town's weaving mill. Werda had been known for centuries for its fine crafts in ceramics and cloth, as well as lace. Oma had worked in the same factory that had once been on the outskirts of the village and was now surrounded by smaller houses and garden plots. It was in the same factory where her husband, Walter, had died crushed under a collapsing loom and cabinet.

At any rate, we were lucky to have an apartment with two bedrooms. The Russian supervised politicians of our town probably assigned it to us because both my parents were teachers and we were willing to share the place with my great-grandmother who would otherwise have nowhere to live. Sadly, no one had heard of insulation and my parents' arguments were clearly heard by all our neighbors. Most of us were embarrassed but had gotten used to these scenes.

"Don't listen, my darling," my favorite person in the whole world said as she tenderly washed my back with an old washcloth soft from years of use.

But I couldn't help hearing. I knew the message of those angry sounds repeated every time my father came to town for a visit. He had been assigned to teach in a school in Goerlitz, a town one day's travel from us. He came home to see me and fight with my mother as often as he could manage.

But this time the shrieking and sobbing did not stop. When I was wrapped in a towel and sitting on Oma's lap near the potbellied stove that heated all our water and the kitchen where we spent most of our time, my dad stormed through the door. His face was red with fury and he stood for a moment to calm down. When he kneeled next to me and took my face in his hands before kissing each of my cheeks, I saw the beginnings of tears in his eyes. Something had changed. He told me he would be back for the next soccer game and quickly left the room. I could hear the outside door close softly. My mother continued to sob.

That night my body feels as though it is tightly wrapped in arms that don't allow movement. The shadow world I now experience is so different from the one I know during a normal day. But even if my body can't move, my mind is free and thoughts roam beyond the boundaries of this ancient room. I float in a joyful dance toward a boundless horizon and experience once more the glory of colors for which I have no name. This other place is where I belong with others like me playing in a field of light and sounds. My attention is suddenly captured by a sense of freedom and movement that suffuses my being. There is no sense of time and I remain suspended in the brilliance of my flight. Perhaps minutes, perhaps hours pass. Dimly, I become aware that someone is holding my body. Shrinking, sinking, I compress myself to fit into Oma's arms that cradle me. Eyes, more violet than blue, twinkle through the wrinkles of her smiling face. She is my Oma and she loves me. I can feel this and know that she is happy I am here.

"She's waking up." This was directed toward my mother who finds no joy in life anymore. It was a long time since my dad had been home for a visit but we'd made plans without him to take the short train ride to Dresden, Saxony's capital, only a score of miles from our town.

The morning was brilliant. Sunshine streamed into the train's windows and fields of yellow blossoms flew past. Clumps of trees, green leaves waving gently in a breeze, housed swarms of birds that took to the air in groups of dozens. I sat next to the window and noticed my reflection, a pale and indistinct version of myself. I stayed steady as the world around me picked up speed.

Mom sat next to me chatting with a woman in the seat across from hers. Neither paid attention to me so I daydreamed while one beautiful field and forest after another streamed past my window. Occasionally, a word or phrase penetrated my thoughts.

"But, you know how they can be. We have our faults, too, I suppose. You have to remember, though, that by nature, men are limited."

My mother's reflection in the window nodded vigorously.

"At first, he swept me off my feet. Then, after Karin was born, he was transferred to teach. That was bad because I missed him so much. But it wasn't until we got married that he drank way too much and every time he came home he'd spend most of his time with friends at their favorite bar."

"Well, you're not the first and you won't be the last."

The rest of their conversation was lost to me when I spotted the skyline of Dresden.

Pulling into the Dresden train station, we saw scores of people hurrying to catch trains or disembarking and rushing to exits. We were swept along with the crowd and excitement helped me keep up with my mother's nearly running feet.

When we finally slowed down and found a bench to sit on, mother asked me again, "Karin, why are we here in Dresden?"

"To shop for material for you to sew a new dress."

"What else?" This said with arched eyebrows.

"To visit the Frauenkirche."

"That's right. And what did I tell you to remember about that church?"

"It was bombed at the end of World War II. I wasn't born yet so I don't remember it but the pictures of it are beautiful. I really like the dome on it. It was called, 'stone bell.'"

"That's right. It had stood for a thousand years before it was destroyed. Even though it was baroque architecture, it was unusual and very ornate. What else do you remember?"

"Well, your mom was here in Dresden when the air raid sirens started. Nobody expected the city to be bombed. People used to call it 'Florence on the Elbe.' There were no soldiers here but the Allies did it anyway."

"That's right. And it just goes to show what the madness of war makes people do."

"But, Mommy, I don't understand why anyone would bomb the 'Church Of Our Lady.' Wasn't it just a place to pray and say thank you to a very nice woman?"

"The religious people say that the church represents the mother of God. You're only five years old and that's way too young to understand these things."

"Why aren't we religious?"

"We're not allowed to be. The people who make the rules now are Communists from Russia and they want everyone to worship only them."

"Not even God?"

"Especially not God."

After a long walk, we were finally able to see the rubble that had once been a place of worship. What remained was still awesome. The huge mound of blackened stones was testimony to the deep wound suffered by people of a once beautiful city. The Frauenkirche, Church Of Our Lady, with its frightful reminder of civilian suffering, stood like an empty shell. But a blackened statue of Martin Luther still stood tall amidst the rubble. Was it hope I felt when I realized not everything was ashes?

Dresden Frauenkirche ruins

It seemed like a long time until we stopped walking. I saw enough gray landscape to last me a very long time. Every street was littered with fallen stones from buildings that had lost all semblance of their former purpose. Interspersed were shops that provided the only relief from drabness. Most apartments on upper floors had windows dressed with white lace curtains.

I was staring up at one of the windows with a particularly beautifully draped lace when I became aware that my mother was no longer at my side. Confused, I retraced my steps. There was no sign of her anywhere.

"Mommy, where are you?"

I kept shouting and turning around. There was no sign of her. Before the tears in my eyes fell to my cheeks, I felt a hand on my right shoulder. Turning in that direction, I looked up and into the face of a man leaning down to get a closer look at me.

"Are you lost?"

"My mommy, I don't see her."

"Here, let me lift you to my shoulders so you can have a look around."

With that, he swung me onto his shoulders and I wrapped my arms around his neck to lace my fingers under his chin. I was instantly comforted and reminded of the many times my father had carried me in just the same way. Walking slowly in the direction I had originally come, I kept shouting and looking around. Finally, my mother emerged from a door leading to a clothing shop. When she followed my voice and finally saw me, her face was a cloud of anger. The man swung me down from his shoulders and I ran into my mother's arms.

"What are you doing with my daughter? She was supposed to follow me into the shop."

"She was lost and looking for you."

"Well, I can't keep track of every move she makes. But, thank you, I guess."

Heading back to the train station, I turned to wave at the kind man who had helped me find my mother. He smiled and turned to walk away.

Chapter 2

My mother, Ella, and I were in the middle of the Atlantic when the fiercest winds in recorded history raised waves that lifted and plunged the *Italia* like a cork in a storm. That was in 1958, a year in which the world was reinventing itself. A year earlier, my mother and I had escaped from East Germany, and after sixteen months of hiding and interrogations in the American zone known as West Germany, we were heading to the United States.

The other storm that was brewing wasn't as apparent. In fact, it was hidden to all but the most perceptive of people. I didn't have a clue.

We landed at a place called Ellis Island after passing a green statue of a lady shrouded in wispy clouds. She wore a crown and held up a torch whose top disappeared into the overcast sky. By then my mother had found me peering over the rail and came to put a slender hand on my shoulder. "What is that?" I asked, pointing to the statue that was quickly disappearing into the mist.

"I don't know but I think she is important." The green lady was the second celebrated woman I had seen. The first one had fallen into a heap of rubble when unchecked insanity had slain her. This woman stood tall and proud.

The bustle and lights of New York were short-lived. After what seemed like endless hours of searching through tiled corridors with domed ceilings for the right train platform, mother finally gave up and sat on our only suitcase, weeping. I had no idea what to do and stood by as dozens of people rushed around us to reach tunnels and trains. Finally, after what seemed like ages, a man noticed and took pity on us. I showed him our tickets and he pointed back in the direction from which we had come. Grateful, I took our tickets back, curtsied, and shook the blackest hand I had ever seen.

The two-day train ride seemed to last forever. With each shriek of the train's whistle, mother jumped in her seat. With each passing mile, the muscles around her mouth and jaw clenched more tightly. Daylight gave way to darkness and then endless plains. If anyone had asked me where we were going, I wouldn't have known what to tell them.

By the time we got to Grand Forks, North Dakota, a new day and a new life had begun. The man I was told to call "Grandpa" in private and "Herr Professor" in public was as silent as my grandmother was talkative on our drive from the station to their house.

It was the first time I had been in a car and the swerving and jerking through traffic made my stomach lurch and settle where it was never intended to be. Squirming in the backseat of the green Edsel, my knitted skirt of leftover yarns, already too short, twisted up on my thighs and invited disapproving stares from Grandma. Grandpa's brows had knitted in what I eventually learned was a rearview mirror. Mother twittered nervously while she skidded back and forth next to me on the plastic-covered bench seat we shared. Each turn seemed sharper than the last until Grandma Mia, tired of competing with the noise of screeching tires, turned to her husband and yelled at him in a language I couldn't understand.

When we walked up the porch steps of a yellow clapboard house on University Avenue and the screen door had banged shut behind us, my mother was crying and Grandma's lips had transformed into a tight line. The scratch on my thigh where Mom had slapped my skirt into obedient folds was getting red and sore. It didn't help to have our cardboard suitcase bump my legs every step I took up unfamiliar stairs. In it was everything we still owned, everything that was left from our past, and I clutched it as though my life depended on not letting go.

"You two will be sleeping in the back bedroom. Put your things in there and wash up for dinner." Grandma pointed me in a direction opposite of where she was headed and I made my way toward an open door at the end of a short hall. Two narrow mattresses in black wooden frames took up most of the room illuminated by a small corner window. Mom, I knew, would want the first bed closest to the door so I dropped the suitcase and made my way to the bed against the far wall. A breeze stirred short curtains as I sat on soft, nubby fabric. Grandpa and my mother's voices carried softly into the bedroom. An occasional sound of clattering dishes came from the kitchen. Nothing else stirred and my mind began to wander to earlier, sweeter times.

It is always the same. The train pulls into the station. I can see people jumping off metal stairs as doors are flung open even before the cars are fully stopped. Shouts and whistles among the clutter of baggage pierce the air as I anxiously scan the milling crowd for a sign of my father. I stand like a tightly wound spring ready to burst free. At last, behind a row of windows in a car near the end of the train, I see the familiar movements I've been waiting for. He is shoving and pushing in his haste to reach the exit. I hold myself back to watch him disregard the stairs and leap from the platform. Suitcase in hand and familiar hat on top of his head, he scans the crowd. Within moments, our eyes meet. We simultaneously explode into motion covering the distance between us in only a few heartbeats. I wrap my arms around his neck as he lifts me up and crushes me to his chest.

The memory leaves sharp edges around my mind, and once again, I stroked the soft cover of my unfamiliar bed. For the hundredth time it occurs to me that I may never see my father again. But, as quickly as it comes, I push the thought back into the shadows of my mind.

Part II

New Beginnings

Chapter 3

The next morning I woke to the clatter of dishes and delicious smells drifting into the room I shared with my mother. Some of them were familiar, like eggs crackling in a pan. Others were more elusive, and one in particular, that I would come to know as the smell of cooking bacon, made my mouth water. Could it really be true that people in my new country ate so much delicious food in one meal?

After breakfast, my mother Ella, found me on the porch rocking in a wicker swing and breathing in the scent of newly mowed lawns. No one had fences here and all the yards ran together: a green patchwork with bunches of colorful flowers and towering trees. Morning sunshine sparkled behind her silhouette but her shadowed face wore a sorrowful look.

With a heavy sigh, she lowered herself slowly onto a bent, metal chair next to me. Her focus was on her hands twisting a handkerchief in her lap. "Uncle Willi is dead. He was found in his office hanging from a rope tied around his neck and slung over a beam in the ceiling. It's actually our fault because we didn't go back to Werda when our one-day pass for travel outside the Soviet Zone expired. Willi, because he works, er, worked for the government is, um, was a perfect example of what happens when someone in a family disobeys. They probably thought he had something to do with our escape. We're now considered enemies of the State." She held a letter and newspaper clipping in my direction. When I reached for them, my hand began to shake. The clipping was a list of names following the bold-lettered word, "Verrater" (traitors). Our names were near the top of the list.

I had no idea that loneliness could feel so huge. It was everywhere: in the air I breathed, and in the darkened shade of every color I saw. My stomach threatened to reject the breakfast I had just eaten.

When I heard Grandpa's footsteps on the floorboards behind me, I got up and met him just inside the screen door. He was part of the rhythm of my days now and had come to get me for my mandatory two hours of piano lessons and two hours of reading English. I had only six weeks to learn my new language before school would start.

"Karin, I'm sorry about your uncle but you can't stop preparing for your future. It's important to be strong."

Piano lessons used to be one hour each day but I spent so much time taking bathroom breaks that Grandpa added the extra hour to my lessons. We sat on the bench in front of the upright piano in what he called the "parlor." The metronome beat a steady rhythm and Grandpa's breath tickled my ear each time he bent into me to reach sheets of music and slap them into place.

"Stop daydreaming!" I tried to focus. "Sit up straight, Karin." I did.

Chapter 4

Between daily English and piano lessons from my new grandfather, I was allowed to go to the park across the street. Even though he was no blood relation, he allowed me to call him "Grandfather" with the understanding that this was a privilege. Today had started out better because I was starting to understand my new language. Grandfather was pleased and Omi (I still missed my Oma, Johanna, but having her daughter, Maria, my Omi, with me helped a lot) had given me a bag of cookies to share with the children I would be seeing. A few of them had begun to stay when I approached. I was less lonely. But too many others hated me for reasons I could not understand. They would not come close to me but taunted me from a distance. They pointed at me and laughed. They would point at me and slap their butts in the universal invitation to do something I only dimly understood. Maybe it was because I didn't speak their language well or that I wore the same clothes every day, strange looking to them. Each day I became increasingly aware of how different I was but I did not understand how that was enough to make people hate me so much.

In spite of the teasing, I loved the park. Birds sang exuberantly and all the shades of green lifted my spirits. It was in the park that I could wander like I had in the park in Werda. Without a specific goal or plan, my thoughts could follow their own direction while my eyes picked up impressions from quivering leaves and sun-dappled grasses.

"Get the Nazi!" I heard a moment before clods of earth hit my back. It didn't hurt that much. But the hurt starting in my heart was spreading to every part of my body. Knowing I wasn't wanted was painful in a way I had never felt. I had no idea what to do.

Most of the kids, even the ones that were willing to play with me, thought I was stupid because I could not completely grasp what they were saying. Still, they tolerated me and that gave me hope. I would just have to find the courage to ask one of them in my broken English just what they meant when they called me a Nazi. I had no idea.

Chapter 5

When everyone had errands to run in town or at the university, I stayed in the house alone. I liked that. It gave me a break from the endless chatter and noise. Grandfather was hard of hearing and loved to watch TV. The news and the *Ed Sullivan Show* were his favorites. No matter where I was in the house or even the yard, I would hear the familiar television voices blasting through my thoughts. Grandmother's favorites were, *Have Gun Will Travel* and *Sea Hunt*. Grandpa did not like my grandmother to watch TV alone because it gave the impression of laziness. That was unacceptable so he pretended to like her favorites as well and they both sat on the couch, often holding hands, and invited further damage to their ears.

More than anything, I wanted to go home to be with my dad. When the letter from him finally reached me after nearly eleven months of inspections and rerouting, it broke my heart. He told me how much he loved me and begged me to come home to Werda. He didn't say how I was supposed to do that. I wanted to — needed to — but I knew that there was no way to go back home.

During the second week of March, my grandmother baked a gorgeous birthday cake for me. Saturday, the twelve girls in my class would join me for an afternoon of games and food. I was nervous about having so many people over but Omi assured me that all would go well on my special day.

I was ready. The paper tablecloth covered a worn workbench my grandmother and I had dragged in from the garage. It was narrow but its length held all the plates, cups, candy, and streamers in splashes of garish colors. Pointed paper hats with stretchy bands that go under the chin spilled their glitter all over the table and rug underneath. Grandma had bought a board game she was told was all the rage with young girls. I had never heard of it. Grandpa had even donated his chessboard for the afternoon convinced that my friends would want to play something intellectually stimulating.

I was nervous. The feathers I had stuck into my make-believe headband were beginning to slip and twist by the time it was noon and I was supposed to welcome my guests. But, the courage I had hoped my feathers would impart began to seem ridiculous. I tore them from my head and slammed the door on my way to the sidewalk in front of our house. Nearly a block away I could see one of the girls I had invited walking sedately toward me in a white lace dress. On her head was what turned out to be a cardboard headpiece wrapped in the same lace as the dress. I had never seen anything so beautiful in my life. I ran to meet Leslie, delighted she had accepted my invitation. Smiling, I led her into the front door and looked back to see if the other girls were far behind. It occurred to me that Leslie might not fit in as well as I at first thought with the other girls that were much more fun loving and, I had to admit, loud. After what seemed like ages, I introduced Leslie to my grandparents and mother who took seats in the overstuffed couch and chairs shoved against walls to make room for my guests. We ate most of my birthday cake and continued with punch and assorted candy. When it became clear that no one else would join us, the adults left the room and convened in the kitchen while Leslie and I looked around for something to do. I opened my gift from her, a beautiful doll that fit into my arms like a real baby and cried when turned upside down. I loved it. When I hugged her showing my thanks, a few tears of gratitude began to form in my eyes but I choked them down along with the tears of rejection threatening to break loose. Leslie seemed to know how I felt and opened a case of

Grandfather's playing cards she found next to his chair.

"Do you know any card games?"

"No. I never learned."

Her face crinkled into a smile and Leslie's eyes sparkled as she settled herself on the floor.

Part III

Too Young to be Old

Chapter 6

"Karin, bring me the mop and broom from next-door. And oh, by the way, did you use the new brush for the toilet in number twenty?"

The motel my grandmother and grandfather bought in Monrovia, California had twenty units. The last two had small kitchens and were monthly rentals. The others had one queen-sized bed or two twins. Weary travelers, most of them in a bad mood, would ring the bell in the tiny reception area at all hours of the day and night. My grandmother, Omi, would get out of bed and throw on her chenille robe before meeting her new guests and taking information in a ledger that took up most of the desktop. Some paid up front, most paid when they left, and a few never paid at all.

Before school, it was my job to help Grandmother change sheets in the units where early risers had already left. Today was midafternoon, Friday. I just got out of school but we had had a full house so Omi needed my help. Coming up was a weekend when the ponies were running and the Santa Anita racetrack was only a few blocks away. Most of our customers were the jockeys and patrons of the track. Some brought their families but most of them were couples looking for a fun weekend and a clean place to spend a night or two. On this particular weekend, in number fourteen, we had a guest staying with his wife and baby. While Grandma and I were cleaning their room, they had asked if I could babysit that same evening.

"She's only twelve. You probably want someone older to look after the baby," Omi answered.

"Actually, I think it's okay. Karin will do a fine job, and besides, the baby will be sleeping the whole time we're gone."

Delighted, I was thrilled to earn my first wages.

Promptly, at 6:30 PM, I knocked on the door and was greeted by a woman transformed from pretty to beautiful. She welcomed me with a bright red-lipped smile and rushed out the door on impossibly high heels while her husband, buttoning his coat, ran to catch up with her. I closed the door behind them and turned my attention to the small child lying in her portable crib.

Almost three hours later, a slamming car door and heavy steps interrupted my thoughts about the chapter I was assigned to read by my English literature teacher.

"Open the goddamn door!" The banging was fierce and loud enough to disturb every tenant. I rushed to open it and he stormed in with a face redder than any I had ever seen and eyes raking every corner of the small room.

"She's not here?" he asked in a frantic voice.

"No, I haven't seen her. I thought you were together."

"If we were together I wouldn't be looking for her, now would I?"

"What happened?" I asked, not really wanting to know.

"That dinner cost me a fortune and, of course, she had to spoil it. Everything was fine until she decided to create a scene about nothing at all." Pouring himself a drink from an amber-colored bottle into a plastic cup I had placed on the nightstand just that morning, he sat on the edge of the bed and motioned for me to sit next to him. As I started to sit at the foot of the queen-sized bed, he reached for my arm and pulled me to the spot he had indicated. "Let me tell you what that bitch said to me."

But, instead of telling me anything, he pulled me backwards and wrapped his right leg around my waist. He cut off my protests with a kiss on my mouth that felt designed to smother me. I was reminded of a time when I was no more than four or five years old when I took a walk near our village gardens.

My memories take me back to a warm summer day in the village that was my first home. My thoughts recall that the sun felt warm on my skin even as the shadows grew long from fences strung along the garden path on which my bare feet kicked up a little dust with each step that took me closer to my family's vegetable patch.

Despite warm sunshine glancing off my head and shoulders and the feel of warm cobblestones under my feet, I suddenly feel chilled as I make my way across the street. Ancient evergreens shelter a cluster of people but I wish to be alone. The old hedge hiding a gravelly path beckons. At least ten feet high, it boasts gnarled branches tangled like the thorn bush surrounding a certain fairytale castle and stands guard over several acres of farm plots with less than fertile soil. Here, I begin my fateful walk. Solitude is already a staple of my days and it is not unusual for me to daydream as I seek oblivion from the grayness of my young East German life.

Just as I am about to stop and take a closer look at a patch of thistles beside the path, a man dressed in black pants and shirt, black boots and black coat steps in front of me. A black hat lowered at a rakish angle across his eyes allows me only one short glimpse of an unfamiliar mouth and chin before he covers my own mouth and eyes with a gloved hand. In one quick, dark motion, he pulls me to the ground at his feet and covers me with his darkly clad body. Groping hands and foul breath invade while his rhythmic panting beats out the tempo of my escaping consciousness.

My next sensation is the warmth of afternoon sunlight filtering through foliage and my lowered eyelids. Small twigs and sharp, dry leaves dig into my bare buttocks while my torn clothing, now pushed under my back in an uncomfortable roll, adds an unnatural arch to my spine. The soreness in my body is fighting a feeling of numbness that sweeps in waves across my limbs and threatens to choke all other awareness. The sticky slime between my legs and on my belly eventually draws my attention and I raise my head to look at the unfamiliar slickness that cools with every breeze penetrating my leafy shelter. I don't know what to do. I want to scream. My mouth opens but no sound comes out. I want my Oma but I can't remember where she is. The loudest noise I can make is the crunch of leaves under my rocking butt and legs. In the distance, I hear old women's voices muffled by the tall hedge separating us. There had been a dark man. My mind tries to remember but only shreds of disconnected images remain. I want to throw up. I don't know what I'm feeling but it is making me sick. I want to run but at the same time, I want to sleep again. It is the voices of my friends muffled by trees and distance that make me move. I can't let them find me like this. What would I tell them? I don't even know myself what has happened to me. I'll walk to the other side of town. I'll get away from everyone and see if I am still somewhere. Even my movements are strange to me and it feels like someone or something besides me is making my body move. My body is a familiar stranger and I am afraid. I have never been so afraid.

I make myself see flowers and butterflies in my mind as I walk across a meadow and undulating hills. My feet choose their own way, and as granite steps loom ahead, I know I have reached the steps that lead to our cemetery on the plateau above. An unusually brilliant place of colorful flowers and soothing scents, this resting place has always seemed like a garden to me. For me, it is a place of love and remembrance and now, a place of peace. I make my way between mounds of earth and wooden crosses to pray. "Please, God, if you can hear a small voice, let me die and come home."

I don't know how long I rest in the quiet place where my ancestors slumber. Long enough to forget why I came.

My one prayer, before memory fails me, is to die.

My wish was not granted. I lived.

My prayer for death was answered by the much more powerful challenge to continue life. The gift in that desperate moment was to live long enough to love and laugh again.

This evening in the Motel Pacifica is not so different. With my mind far away as my body is struggling to free itself, only the voice of rage can penetrate.

"You fucking whore! Get the hell out of here!" With that ringing in my ears I was able to gather myself and run past the furious woman who was already hurtling her purse at the man who had not yet found his voice. "You pig!" I heard behind me as I ran toward the front door of the office. There was no way to explain what had happened so I straightened my clothes and entered the living room calmly where Grandpa sat in his overstuffed chair. From the kitchen came my mother and grandmother's voices.

In the room I shared with my mother, I sat on my bed hoping nothing would come of the rage I had heard just minutes before.

Then I heard it again. "That little whore! Get her out here! I want some answers!"

Mother pushed herself through a small crack in the door and looked at me without flinching. "What have you done, Karin?"

"Nothing, Mommy," I answered in a shaky voice. "I didn't do anything."

"Then why is that crazy woman screaming at us? Come out here right now and explain what happened."

We moved down the corridor, my mother behind me with a ready shove to move me along. In the living room, Grandfather sat in his accustomed chair and looked on as Omi ushered the red-faced woman from the office into our living room.

"Now calm down and tell us exactly what you think Karin did."

As she laid eyes on me, the woman's rage peaked again; her voice rose to an unbelievable pitch as she explained that she had come to her room to find me seducing her husband and that we were rolling on the bed holding on to each other. As she spoke, her eyes found my face and I felt as though they might burn into my heart.

Turning to me, Grandmother asked, "What happened?"

"He came home early and grabbed me. I tried to get away but I couldn't."

Now the fury found my grandmother. "Look at her! Look at her!" Her arm and pointed finger were only inches from me.

"That girl barely turned twelve and you are blaming *her* for what your husband did? How dare you! If you're not gone within the hour, I will call the police and turn you both in for rape!"

It was a moment of great rejoicing. Omi had stood up for me. She defended me. She believed me.

From Grandfather's corner chair, I heard his voice: "And so it begins."

Chapter 7

The school year had ended and I had free time when I wasn't helping Omi clean motel rooms. Grandpa was watering the lawn in front of the office, a look of contentment on his face. His green lawn and brilliant rose bushes were his pride and joy. Sunshine lit his water spray and made it look like crystals floating in the air. My shorts were snug around my bare legs and a new t-shirt hung loosely over my budding breasts. Everyone said I was much too young to develop breasts but here they were. Most of the time I was uncomfortable and having to wear a bra felt awkward. I was not thrilled.

"Grandpa, can I help you in the garden?"

"No, I'm finished, but we can walk to Foster's Freeze and I'll buy you an ice cream."

What a wondrous moment. He had seldom bought me anything and something as frivolous as ice cream was impossibly special. I had no money of my own so I had not even considered going across the street to the brightly lit building where lines of people stood every day to savor the cones of sweet delight. Sometimes they even had sprinkles.

Proudly, I walked across the street next to the statuesque man whose bearing left no one in doubt that he was a man of substance. This was my grandfather, the man my grandmother still called "Herr Professor" even at home. I could count on the fingers of one hand the times I had heard her call him

"Joseph."

Behind the small window, a young man, with a white cap sitting precariously on bright red hair, asked me what I wanted. What could I say? "Ice cream, please." That was obvious. Beside me, Grandpa leaned down and said, "A double vanilla cone dipped in chocolate." Chocolate!

The same evening my mother, grandmother, and grandpa sat in the small living room and watched *Gunsmoke* and *Sea Hunt* before the two women went into the kitchen to clean dinner dishes. The swinging door creaked on its hinges as it swung back and forth before settling into its almost level closed position. Their voices and the sound of rattling dishes were muffled when I settled myself at Grandpa's feet, a place I often occupied during evenings when we watched TV together.

I yawned when another commercial interrupted *The Ed Sullivan Show*. Only the gray shades undulating across the screen lit the living room. Electricity was never wasted. When Grandpa asked me to change the channel, I scooted across the rug and twisted the dial.

"That's it," came his voice, more gentle than I had heard in a long time.

Scooting backwards and leaning into his knees again, I looked up into his face, pleased that he was so nice. As I turned back to the TV, a hand patted my back and slid down below my waist. Dumbstruck, not knowing what to do, I sat as still as I could, barely breathing. Then the hand slid lower, into my panties. I started to pull away just as another hand clamped around my waist and pulled me back. This time between his knees. Imprisoned in that bony embrace, I looked toward the kitchen door and the voices escaping through brightly lit cracks.

If I called out, I was sure there would be trouble. What was happening was all wrong but I wasn't quite sure about just how wrong. Was I to blame? Had I done something I shouldn't have? And what about Omi? By the time the hand found the most private part of my body, I was more afraid than I ever remembered being.

When my mother burst into the room, she was laughing at something my grandmother had said. When she saw me and Grandfather sitting in our accustomed places watching television, she smiled. At that moment, I vowed that I would never do or say anything that would take that smile off her face.

It wasn't the last time that "Herr Professor" touched me. It stopped only when mother moved us into an apartment we shared with her boyfriend.

Part IV

Love?

Chapter 8

"Aw, Ella. Why do you have to change your mind again? You either want to marry me or you don't. Don't make it so hard on everyone."

"You just don't understand, Knut. This isn't easy for me."

"I know that and it's not going to get any easier the longer you wait. I'd like to have a proper wedding but if you don't we can just go to court and have a judge marry us."

"I know that but I'm just not ready."

Knut stormed out the door of our one-bedroom apartment like so many others had before him. I was thirteen years old now and had watched my mother through the ups and downs of one relationship after another. The past two years had been especially turbulent because none of the men my mother liked wanted to marry her and the others had unforgiveable flaws.

I desperately wanted her to marry somebody. Not the politician from Arkansas who had driven to North Dakota to woo her after reading an ad my grandfather had published in the personals. Not the businessman from Maine who had come to see her and convinced her to move us to his hometown. After a two-day train ride that took us within eyesight of our destination, Mother changed her mind and we boarded the next train back. I liked him.

There were others but none of them made much of an

impression on me. Everett, the mechanic, was okay and my mother was giddy in love with him. But, he was not thrilled about inheriting a child, me, and avoided commitment. But there had to be someone.

Mother and I stayed close until she met Knut. He was one of her customers at Glendale Federal Savings and Loan where she worked as a teller. Knut, like us, was an immigrant from Germany. Berlin, to be exact. An odd man. A tool and die maker, short, with a lisp and slightly crossed eyes. None of these things taken by themselves were particularly off-putting but together they made a singularly poor impression. The one attribute he possessed was a kind heart. Also, he loved my mother to distraction. Never one to make choices easily, Mother had been waffling about her commitment to him since she had reluctantly made it. I suppose Grandfather was fed up with her whining and finally insisted that she marry Knut. He probably felt that any man with a steady job who loved my mother was better than her continued affairs that inevitably left her in various states of misery.

Knut waited patiently for months while my mother accepted and then turned down his proposals of marriage more times than any of us can remember. During these various episodes of an off-again on-again relationship, my mother managed to put together a wedding outfit of sorts, just in case. We were ready for the big event and waiting only for my mother's final capitulation. Grandpa, realizing she once again worked herself into a state of immobilization, called up on a Friday evening and said he was taking all of us, that is, Knut, Mother, Grandmother, and me to the Los Angeles courthouse on Monday where the marriage would finally take place and give the rest of us a break from their drama.

True to his word, Grandpa picked us up and we drove toward the hub of Los Angeles on the Golden State Freeway. Mother was having mood swings in the backseat next to me. I looked out the car window at palm trees and houses bathed in sunshine. It was a glorious day and what I hoped would be the beginning of a calm and peaceful life.

The Los Angeles courthouse was a popular place where couples without much money or time came to get married. After we reached it and joined the end of a long line of couples waiting to be married by someone behind the desk at the end of the hall, my mother broke out in a wailing singsong expertly modulated to give her voice the best effect from the natural acoustics of the large, domed atrium in which we waited. Finally, too embarrassed to wait with us any longer, Knut threatened to leave. Grandpa turned to me, his face a stony mask and told me to keep my mother in line, by force if necessary. Wheeling about, he dragged Knut aside and whispered a few words into that man's ear. Both came back and stood rigidly next to us until the next gut-wrenching sob escaped my mother. By that time, Omi had moved as far away from us as she could and pretended she was in no way related to our lunatic group. I was ready to run out of the building but was restrained by the meager hope that somehow things would turn out all right.

The mask on Grandpa's face began to crack and he whirled on my mother while hissing words escaped through clenched teeth. He grabbed her arm and dragged her to the corner of the huge hall where she, stunned into silence, checked from the corner of her eyes to see who was watching her drama unfold. Most of the other people, though, were too involved in their own impending marriages to pay her much mind and she turned her attention to Grandpa again. Omi and I waited in embarrassed silence next to Knut while Grandpa talked to and shook my mother. Finally, they returned and we all stood silently in line and occasionally shuffled another step closer toward the man behind the desk.

When the moment arrived and the man behind the desk had read all the legal mumbo jumbo from the paper in his hands, Mother refused to say, "I do." Long moments stretched into painful minutes as my mother, her mouth set in a grim line, squeezes huge tears out of her eyes. I was ready to scream.

Knut looked on adoringly, his victory at hand. Omi was turned away from all of us and Grandpa trembled with rage. The official had also had enough and warned that he will ask only one more time whether or not she will take Knut to be her lawfully wedded husband. Grandpa growls "yes she will" and grips her arm painfully until she makes a sound that, by consensus, is taken to mean agreement. We hurriedly exited through massive doors dragging my mother in our wake. Outside, someone takes a photo of our miserable party and we renegotiate the city toward our new home, a triplex in Glendale.

Mother continues her tantrums and for the first week of her marriage refuses to let Knut sleep with her. There is only one bedroom and mother insisted that I sleep with her while Knut occupied the living room couch that is actually intended to be my bed. Their endless bickering and crying is almost unbearable. Night after night, the tedium of their drama engulfs us until, finally, my mother gives in, and I am relegated to the couch while Knut, in gleeful anticipation, prepares for nuptial bliss.

The rages continue. Mother finally has someone in her life who she can control, utterly. She is intent on making Knut pay for all the suffering inflicted on her by life. Endless cycles of pain, humiliation, and depression are becoming the norm. Both of them fight with each other and compete as to who can endure more pain before striking out. More often than not, I become the focus of their love/hate. It was my fault that mother didn't love him or my fault that he felt disrespected. Therefore, it was my fault that their lives didn't work. But we struggled on, convinced that if we just held on, somehow things would change. They never did.

Chapter 9

During the second semester of Ms. Wilson's ninth grade art class, the principal, Mr. Walker, came into the studio classroom with a new student. He introduced Jerry and told us that he was transferring from Page, Arizona. Unruly, dark blond curls topped his head in unrestrained disarray and clothes that had an ease about them nearly to the point of shabby hung on his tall frame. Icy blue eyes softened whenever he smiled. If there had been a cave nearby, Jerry could have dragged me into it and I would have stayed there with him forever. Instead, he shifted in his seat and looked away. I turned, too embarrassed to have been caught by his look. Did I imagine the tentacles of his thoughts brushing the back of my neck?

Even though it was two weeks from the time I first saw him, I still felt as though I had contracted a disease. I was alternately euphoric and desperate to fill the emptiness inside my heart. I sweated, I giggled uncontrollably, and I grew dark circles under my eyes from sleepless nights thinking about him.

It didn't help that it became obvious after only a few days that he was the most talented artist any of the students or even Ms. Wilson had ever seen. He could draw, he could paint, he could sculpt. All of it effortlessly.

I, on the other hand, was a good student in history, sociology, even English. It took a while but at some point, I stopped dreaming and got back to living my life with my books and lonely walks.

What became clear to me was my loneliness. It had never hurt so much as when I imagined myself with someone who accepted me and perhaps even loved me. Although men had often paid attention to me, it was usually not the kind of attention that made me feel cared for and special.

Over time, it became clear that Jerry was no more mainstream than me and yet his aloneness seemed to be a choice rather than a circumstance. Because he preferred to be alone while I craved acceptance, he seemed like a tower of strength to me. While I studied and struggled with the issues of social and interpersonal relationships, Jerry was fascinated by science with a virtual disregard for the feelings and actions of others. His art was equally divorced from their opinions. He valued animals, any animal, more highly and made no excuses.

My locker was just outside the studio and I exchanged one set of books for another before slamming the locker door in place and giving my lock a last, forceful spin. When I turned around to hurry to my next class, I crashed head on into his chest. Embarrassed, laughing, blood rushing to my face, I stammered irrelevancies for only a moment before falling silent under the impact of his stare. Neither of us had words. We didn't need any. I was looking at the rest of my life.

Chapter 10

"You Gott verdammte bastard!" The shrieking voice was my mother's and the sound of breaking dishes was exactly that: a china platter hitting the floor after splitting in half on Knut's head. The turkey that had once lain in repose slithered in its own greasy juices down the front of Knut's shirt.

"Stop it, Ella! Please. Stop this."

I had no idea what started this row but it was expected. Whenever Mother felt under pressure, like on those rare occasions when she prepared a meal, her anxiety surpassed her ability to control her outbursts. I was watching the scene from our den, glad that for once I had not been the cause of their fight. While Knut went upstairs to shower and change, mother threw the turkey into the sink before sitting down at the kitchen table. Staring out the window, my mother allowed more tears to fall from her eyes. When I asked her if I could help, there was no reply.

"Is it okay if I take some mashed potatoes?"

Still no reply, so I helped myself to a bowl of the creamy mixture and retreated into the den to eat my Thanksgiving dinner.

It had definitely been different last year. Thanksgiving at Jerry's house had been a raucous affair with mountains of food on the dining room table that had been pulled out to its max.

An assortment of card tables had also been arranged where space allowed and relatives as well as friends sat wherever they found a vacant seat. Thanksgiving was exactly that, a time of giving thanks for the feast that marked a turning point in the earliest years of this country. A time when starvation was avoided by the kindness of strangers who would eventually have reason to regret their generosity. That day, though, was a day of gratitude for the abundance that could be shared with family and friends. The noise made conversation difficult and Jerry and I had made our way to the patio between the house and garage.

"When are you leaving?"

"Not until Saturday, day after tomorrow. I have to be in Fort Benning by Monday morning and my flight to Nam leaves Tuesday."

Vietnam. No one had heard of it until the military involvement of the United States in 1954. It was called a "conflict" instead of "war," a distinction I have never understood. It claimed hundreds of thousands of lives and left many more in desperate ruins. Yes, it was war and Jerry had volunteered to fight.

I was on the opposite side of political opinion. Alienated from Jerry, I couldn't let myself feel the real terror at the thought of his leaving for nearly certain death. Red earth, jungle terrain, a place on the globe few people had heard of and even fewer had thought about.

Images of horrific pain and ruined bodies flooded TV screens in virtually every home in the United States. Talking heads fought to convince the country of their point of view. A division had developed in a heretofore cohesive society. America was divided between trust in our government and outrage at its presumptions. A young generation set out to prove its independence and openly voice its grievances.

At UCLA, shouts of "peace" and "stop the war" accompanied

hundreds of raised hands with fingers spread. It became recognized as the peace sign of what was becoming known as the vocal group of "peaceniks."

The din of shouting voices assaulted my ears as bodies pressed against mine, driven by an armed line of uniformed riot police. Nearing the Jans steps at the end of the original university quad, the shouting students, including me, were driven closer and closer into the funnel of walls leading toward the steps that led downward into other open spaces. Next to me, another protester handed me a pen and told me to write a number on the palm of my hand. On his palm was the number for an underground contact lawyer for those who were arrested. Driven ever farther toward Jans steps, I looked up into the second-story windows of Royce Hall on my left and the beautiful original library on my right. That library had often been my sanctuary. I loved to spend peaceful hours inside its giant halls of seemingly endless stacks of books.

Today the library was not a sanctuary but a cauldron of agitated bodies, many sitting on windowsills or leaning precariously into unsupported space. They lent their voices to those of us on the ground.

Suddenly, all movement stopped and a voice carried over a loudspeaker told us to desist. We were told, "A spokesperson from your group is meeting with the chancellor right now. No one will be arrested if you disperse and return to your classes."

A dull roar of grumbles could be heard all around but the momentum had been broken. Some students remained in small groups to discuss our effort to have a voice against the atrocities we felt were being illegally imposed on people half a world away. Others, like me, went to our scheduled classes and listened to professors share their opinions about what students were doing at UCLA and many other campuses across the country. Some decided to stick to their scheduled lectures, an admittedly safer choice in terms of their careers. Those lecture halls were nearly empty.

On April 30, 1970, President Richard M. Nixon announced that it had become necessary to draft an additional 150,000 men for expansion into Cambodia. The unrest on campuses across the nation escalated into violent protests. By Monday, May 4 of the same year, four unarmed students at Kent State University were killed by members of the nine hundred Ohio National Guardsmen stationed on that campus.

Part V

Moving Forward

Chapter 11

"Get back into this house!" I was running down the eight steps from the front door to the street below where two friends were waiting in Phillip's car. He and Horst were friends from high school. We were going to meet more friends at Danielle's house to catch up on the changes in our lives since graduating from North Hollywood High School. Danielle was studying medicine at Berkeley and was home for a long weekend. Ronnie was in veterinary school and would be moving to Spain to continue his studies. Danny was already in graduate school with a focus on existential philosophy. This was a rare opportunity to spend an afternoon and evening together before resuming our busy lives.

Mother and Knut had told me I could not leave the house. They had been drinking and were upset with me about something I could not figure out. It had become their habit to close all the curtains when Knut came home from work, earlier on weekends. Then they would start drinking. Sometimes the light from the TV would illuminate their silhouettes but most often no lights or TV were on. Drinking and fighting took place in darkness.

On this particular day, they had started drinking earlier than usual and I was determined to spend time with my friends. A particularly unfortunate congruence of events.

By the time I reached the bottom of the steps, both my mother and Knut were stumbling down as well. Horst had opened the back door of the car and it was the target I was aiming at. Knut got there first. Positioned in front of the door, he pushed me back each time I tried to get around him and into the backseat. It was a stalemate until my mother grabbed my arms from the back and pinned me down so Knut could push and slap me.

My body found strength from resources I did not know I had. I pushed against my mother and sent her sprawling into the street. Whirling around, I pushed Knut so hard that he fell on top of the trunk of the old Ford. This gave me enough time to jump into the backseat and scream, "Floor it!"

Mother's mood swings had gotten worse. She never seemed happy anymore. When she wasn't screaming, she was crying or buried behind a wall of silence. Once in a while, the woman I thought was my real mother would peek out from behind her mask of rage and sorrow to ask for a hug or kiss. I missed her terribly.

Neighbors and people we encountered together in public never suspected that behind the saccharin smile and effusive behavior raged a terrifying woman.

When I returned home that evening, they were sitting in the darkened den. Two empty gallon bottles of vodka sat on the table in front of them. In a voice louder than I had intended, I said, "I'm moving out."

Chapter 12

The Vietnam War was still raging at its most horrifying pitch when Jerry's mother and I drove to the L.A. airport to pick him up. He had served two consecutive terms on the front lines in Vietnam and was coming home. When we spotted each other outside the arrival gate, all three of us closed the distance in moments that seemed to last forever. The smell assaulted me before we were close enough to touch. Pungent, raw, rotten. It was the smell of the jungle, a dark place of lush greens and blood.

He was tired, more tired than I had ever seen anyone. The dark circles under his eyes reached down past his cheekbones and made his eyes seem bright and feverish. His easy smile had changed, too. Somehow frozen and plastered awkwardly where his lips had once been. It wasn't until his arms drew me into a familiar embrace that I fully recognized the man that had once been the boy I knew.

He wanted only three things in his stateside life: a motorcycle, a fabulous sound system, and me. He brought only two things with him from Asia: a camera and his beloved papasan chair. He was home. He was safe. But he was not sound.

He jerked and ducked behind the nearest pillar when a van dropping airline passengers off backfired.

"Sorry," he mumbled when we continued toward the elevator that would take us to the level where our car was parked.

Jerry wanted to go to the Montana high country where he was born and where his paternal grandmother still lived. I took time off from my jobs cleaning houses and babysitting for two families. UCLA, on the quarter system, was between sessions, so, Jerry and I packed my red VW "bug" and headed for Kalispell.

The city of Kalispell and the surrounding mountains were breathtaking. We spent a night with Jerry's grandmother, Hulda, but, more often than not, we camped. Hulda had baked a rhubarb pie for us, a recipe she had brought with her from her native Norway. I marveled that this tiny woman, four feet and three inches, had given birth to no fewer than fifteen children. The smallest was born fourteen pounds and two ounces.

That was not the only remarkable thing about Jerry's grandmother. She and her husband had emigrated from Norway when starvation drove them to seek a better life in America. They settled in the mountain country of Montana that resembled the home they left in Scandinavia.

Jerry and I now sat with her in the small cabin that had been her home since then. We asked her to tell the story of meeting with a bear in the backyard, which I could see from the small window near my chair. It was a well-known tale in the family but I wanted to hear it from Hulda herself.

"It was cold," she started with an accent that left no doubt about her first language. "We'd been losing a lot of chickens and Uwe (her husband) had gone higher into the mountains to hunt. He'd been gone almost a week and I was worried. The snow was deep even in our yard and it was dangerous up there. Besides, we were running out of food and I had youngsters to feed. That morning I went out to check on the few hens we had left and saw a huge bear near the hen house. I yelled at him to get away and I waved my arms so he could see I meant it. But he wouldn't budge. After a while, I was mad and got my axe from the woodpile. I gave him one more chance to leave my hens alone but he didn't care about my yelling. So, I walked up to him and started hitting him with the axe. He was kind of hard to kill but I managed. The bear hide nearly froze while I was skinning him and it was a good thing he was only a big brown bear and not a grizzly. Uwe came home with a deer a few days later and we ate well the rest of the winter."

The next day Jerry and I drove my little red car into those very same mountains as far as the narrow trail would allow. We had to hike the rest of the way to the top and he showed me how to take uneven steps to confuse any bears or other predators about who and where we were.

"Keep to your left," he said softly when we were near the top. A few steps later, Jerry turned me back in the direction we had just come and silently pointed. I saw something disappear into the bush I had brushed with my hand only moments earlier.

"What is that?" I asked in a shaky voice.

"You don't want to know."

A few more yards and we were on top of the hillock we'd been climbing. A flat rock served as a seat where we ate the sandwiches Hulda had made for us. Suddenly, Jerry froze with his sandwich halfway to his mouth. Instead of the sandwich, he put his finger across his lips in the sign for silence.

"See that tree in the middle of the clearing about halfway down this side of the hill?" he whispered. I looked where he pointed and saw an enormous dark trunk pointing straight into the sky. Suddenly, what I thought was the top of a tree turned ninety degrees and I recognized a nose that was now twitching in our direction.

"That's a grizzly and he's smelling lunch. And I don't mean just our sandwiches. Get down slowly, and when we're over the crest, walk the way I showed you as fast as you can back to the car."

Once inside, the engine screaming, we flew down that mountain, a red streak among towering pines.

Jerry and I drove back to Los Angeles with a stop in Las Vegas. We called both our mothers and told them that if they wanted to, they could come to LV the next day to see us get married.

The little white chapel. No cameras, please. No flowers either. Mother was bringing a bunch of roses from her garden. No, no piped music. Jerry could not stand the idea of a crowd or anything more than a simple "I do." The only sounds that accompanied our vows were my mother's sobs.

Chapter 13

It took another year before I finished my bachelor's degree in history at UCLA. During that time Jerry and I lived in a tiny apartment near Griffith Park. We had no furniture so we spent a lot of time in the evenings sitting on the floor and talking. I would tell him about my classes that day and he would occasionally reveal how difficult it was for him not to be able to relate to the men he worked with on construction sites.

One of the things we discussed often was his continued drug use. In Vietnam, many soldiers stayed drunk or high most of the time. Jerry was no exception. He had come home with a habit that dominated our lives.

"Karin, I want you to try this powder I got from one of the guys at work. You should have some idea of what this is like. If you don't love it, I'll throw it all out and never use again."

He showed me how to hold one nostril closed while inhaling forcefully with the other. The line of fine powder disappeared into one end of the straw he held and into my nose through the other end. "Try not to sneeze or cough. You'll lose it that way."

I didn't lose any and settled back against the wall. Nothing. "What's going to happen?" I asked.

"I don't know. Everybody is different."

I was not reassured but I knew that Jerry would never let anything bad happen to me. So, I waited. It could have been five minutes or fifty when it occurred to me that I had no concept of time. In fact, I was getting hungry and thirsty. But not just that, the blue carpet we were sitting on seemed bluer and the white walls brighter. It was curious that I hadn't noticed that before. My balance was off when I tried to get up off the floor and Jerry laughed while pushing me into an upright position. The short walk into the kitchen was an adventure. It was tiny but the cabinets kept receding so that each step brought me only inches farther along.

My coordination was sadly lacking and Jerry poured me a glass of milk while I watched. When I picked it up to take a sip, it changed to an amazing fluorescent green.

"Oh my God!" I heard myself say.

True to his word, Jerry dumped the rest of his stash into the toilet and flushed it down.

Chapter 14

Right after my graduation, Jerry and I packed up our few belongings and drove to Colorado. He couldn't stand the traffic and crowding in Southern California and I desperately wanted a change. A new beginning. A new everything.

"The geese need feeding." Dreaded words from Dotty. Every time I went even near the backyard, the damn goose would charge as fast as she could. Whenever I was too slow or burdened with groceries she would get a bite in. My legs and butt were bruised and I hated her almost as much as she hated me. It didn't help that she could stretch her head almost to my shoulders when she was in a particularly foul mood.

Everyone, including Jerry, found this standoff hilarious and I really could hardly complain since we were living in his Uncle Frank and Aunt Dotty's unfinished basement. It was an arrangement we would all have to tolerate until the 140-year-old cabin in Bakersfield was cleaned out. It belonged to the family who employed Frank and Jerry as drivers for their propane delivery company. So far, the change from city life to neighbors no closer than a mile had not been easy.

There were good times, too. The community was a tightknit group of families with many of its members related and a long history of occupying that part of the Four Corners area. They really did not love newcomers but were willing to help us "city folks" when we needed it.

We were greeted by a "welcome wagon" the first month we were in the Durango area. I had never heard of such a tradition until a group of five women stood at my door with arms full of baked goods and several bottles of homemade elderberry wine. The afternoon weather was mild and I had just finished putting up red and white checked curtains covering kitchen cupboards. The old log cabin had once been converted from a Wells Fargo stagecoach stop into a residence where Jerry's boss's wife's grandmother had been born. Now it was ours for a nominal rent until we could afford a place of our own. I don't remember much of what happened after we started drinking but it must have been fun. Every woman's make-up was smeared from tears of laughter and no one was steady on their feet when they left.

I took what I thought was a quick nap and didn't wake up until after dark when Jerry came home from work and shook my shoulder. "Had fun, eh?" I could only shake my head yes and went back to sleep.

Less than a year later, my grandmother died. The cancer had spread throughout her abdomen, and by the time it was diagnosed, it had become inoperable. None of the other losses left me with such a sharp pain that it took my breath away. Even though escaping from East Germany had meant I could never see my family again, I knew they were alive somewhere. This was different. The woman I called Omi had been a constant my entire life. She had cooked my favorite meals for me, spent endless hours telling me about our family and how life was even before I was born, and she had never stopped loving me. To know she was gone, to know I would never see her again was like falling into a black hole with no bottom.

Her last gift to me was enough money to buy a three-acre plot of land between Durango and Bayfield. There was an extra $150 to buy an old, gutted trailer that Jerry and I planned to refurbish. Later, we would add rooms as we could afford.

Fall set in early that year and our fourteen-foot trailer was still nothing but a shell. I had a cooktop to prepare meals and we sat on our trailer steps to eat. Our bedroom was a loft consisting of a plywood floor with a mattress and a four-foot span to the ceiling. We climbed up there every night and added more and more blankets as the Colorado nights grew colder.

We had a toilet but no walls. No way to heat or contain warmth in our little trailer. Almost all of our belongings, some furniture, and many boxes were piled high under a huge blue tarp next to the front door. None of this would have been impossible to manage under normal circumstances. But, circumstances were anything but normal. Jerry was getting more and more restless. He had quit his job delivering propane gas and money was running out. Even though I now taught high school in Bayfield, my salary was not enough to support our needs.

Jerry jumped every time he heard a loud noise. Once, when we were getting into our red '57 Chevy pickup on our way into town, the storm that had been threatening broke over our heads. The clap of thunder and lightning delighted me. I felt like I was in a primordial world. Jerry was in a different world.

"Jerry? Where are you?" There was no sign of him. A few minutes later, he stood up. Clearly, he had thrown himself on the ground. He got behind the wheel but never said a word.

That's when I began to realize that Jerry and I were growing further apart, not closer. TV news and papers had just started talking about a cluster of symptoms and behaviors soldiers exhibited even after years back home. It explained why he took frequent "hunting trips" that would last days, sometimes weeks. It also explained the mood changes and silences that had grown between us.

The pressures were building. I was fed up with life in a cold trailer and having to climb a ladder to get to our loft bed. What made it worse was that I was pregnant. Although Jerry and I were delighted that we would have a child, I was increasingly grumpy and anxious. We had tried over two years to get pregnant. Finally, we were tested and told that neither one of us could have a child. When that turned out to be false, we were ecstatic. But it meant more pressure, less time and much less patience.

My breaking point came when I waddled my nine-month pregnancy to our tarped belongings and lifted the plastic in search for a pot I needed. Jerry was gone on one of his hikes and I had no idea when he would be home. The movement and sound of a rattle triggered an immediate response in me. Without my conscious will, my body hurdled itself backwards four plus feet. Still upright but precariously balanced, my enormous belly pulled one way while my flailing arms churned to keep me from falling. Once I righted myself, I rushed to the ancient phone I kept on the floor just inside the door. Our phone line was shared by three other households and one of them, our nearest neighbor a mile and a half down the road, was using it.

"Help! I've got a snake in my yard! It's in my stuff! Please help."

"I'll send Al right away. He's out in the yard working on the car."

Within fifteen minutes, Al was walking toward where I sat on my doorstep, a shotgun cradled in the crook of his arm.

"I hear you've got a problem guest."

I nodded and pointed to the blue tarp. In a shaky voice, I explained what I thought I saw.

"Well then, let's see what's in that perfect little hiding place you've built."

With that, Al lifted one side of the plastic with his shotgun until half the pile of my belongings was exposed. When nothing moved, he banged his gun against one of the boxes, and sure enough, there was movement.

"I may hit something you don't want hit. I'll try not to but it's up to you if you want me to get rid of this critter."

"Definitely."

"Okay then."

Moments later, a sharp bang shattered the air.

"Got'er." With that, Al bent down and picked up the snake just below its shattered head. With his arm straight out, the snake was long enough for its tail to touch the ground.

"Mind if I take this one home? It'll make a nice belt."

Part VI

More New Beginnings

Chapter 15

Two months after our baby, Kelsy, was born, Jerry and I sold our three acres and trailer shell in Colorado and moved to New Mexico. We just couldn't endure another cold winter. The trailer had been built for a much warmer climate so that the lack of insulation made living in it feel like living in a refrigerator. But, it was cheap and after paying for three acres to put it on, it was all we could afford. Besides, Jerry had never gotten around to putting a skirt on it to keep wind and cold temperatures from freezing the floors.

Jerry had told me the whole previous year that he would enclose the bottom of our home with logs he would cut from timber we had growing all around us. He had even cut and trimmed all the wood he would need. But it lay in a pile behind the house as seasons came and went. New Mexico seemed like the perfect answer.

More and more frequently, Jerry fell asleep during the day. We didn't talk much anymore either. We didn't seem to have much to talk about and Jerry withdrew into his own thoughts more and more. He had no explanation for his increasing nightmares or the times he choked or unwittingly hit me while we slept uneasily next to each other. Only when he screamed orders in his sleep like "Gooks on your left! Down! Down! Fire!" did it become obvious that Vietnam was not in the past. The afternoon, in August, when rain pounded on our driveway and lightning struck too close for comfort in our front yard, Jerry woke up from one of his naps screaming.

He looked at me but said nothing. Only his eyes spoke of memories too painful for words.

That same evening we decided to move and make a new start. Somewhere where Jerry's individualistic and socially indifferent nature would not bother anyone. A place where people would appreciate his kind and loyal heart, his love of family and friends. Somewhere where he could paint and sculpt to make a living without punching a time card. Somewhere where he could look out a window without seeing civilization.

Orogrande was a tiny town of sixty-five souls halfway between El Paso and Alamogordo. There was a gas station and a saloon. The saloon did a thriving business.

"There are a lot of people walking across the backyard near the river." I was gazing out my kitchen window watching stragglers keep close to the river just back of the yard that was mostly sand and weeds.

"Don't worry about them. They're Mexicans going north to try to find jobs. They won't hurt us. They're just looking to make a living."

I sat at the table we had brought from our trailer home and sipped a cup of coffee. None of these travelers had ever bothered us. They moved in the early dawn hours and in the late hours of evening. None seemed to carry much baggage. Just a few sacks, mostly plastic. They had less than we did even though our house was a clapboard antique over one hundred years old.

I thought about that a long time. It was important to remember that I had started life in East Germany and that my mother and I had escaped to the United States for the opportunity to have a better life. Even though it had not been easy, I had adjusted and graduated from a leading university. I was a teacher and a housewife. I had a home and a husband who loved me. I looked out my window again. No one was in sight.

I had not gotten a teaching job in Alamogordo even though I had applied months before Jerry, our baby, and I moved into the area. I had not quite given up hope, but just in case, I also put in an application on Holloman Air Force Base to administer an extension university program. Money was tight. We were running out of the small profit we had made in selling our place in Colorado. Jerry wasn't working either. He spent more and more time taking long walks in the New Mexico desert. He wouldn't talk about what he was thinking or feeling or why he had stopped looking for a job.

Kelsy's crib was at the foot of our bed in the tiny room that also held our queen-sized mattress. It was on the floor shoved against the only window. When I rolled over on my left side, I could look out because it was eye level. When the house was built, windows were low to the floor, and for me, it was a perfect view of golden sands and blue skies.

When Jerry joined me in bed on a particularly beautiful fall evening, he turned to me and smiled. When he took me into his arms, I snuggled against his chest and felt the familiar feeling I always had when he held me close. I was safe.

"Would you like to make another baby?"

I was shocked by his question. We were barely able to pay our bills so another child had not even occurred to me.

"I think we need to wait until we're more financially stable. We don't even have the space for another child until you finish converting the porch into a second bedroom."

Jerry nodded, rolled over, and we went to sleep.

The next morning I woke when Jerry's hand brushed over my breasts. It was too heavy so I pushed at it to get it away from me. It wouldn't budge. Fully awake now, I opened my eyes and looked down.

"Nooooo! Jerry! Help!"

The huge iguana turned his head and blinked. I was staring into the face of a creature that was unfazed by my outburst. I was frozen in place. No more sound escaped my mouth. I had no idea what prompted the green intruder to move but he made an about-face and scurried onto the bed on Jerry's side before plopping on the floor and disappearing.

When I dared to get out of bed, the creature was nowhere to be found. Neither was Jerry.

Chapter 16

I waited. And waited. Two months later, there was a letter waiting for me at the "watering hole." That's what everyone called the only business in town. It was the only place with an address. Everyone got their mail there.

Walking the dusty trail home, tears began to flow. I had not given up hope that this was just another one of Jerry's long treks into the far reaches of the desert surrounding us. The return address on the envelope was Montana.

I took a day off from my work waiting on tables at the only small coffee shop outside Orogrande. There was no point in going because I could not have served anyone even to save my life. I fed Kelsy and put her into her crib with her toys. There weren't many but they kept her busy and happy.

Back at my kitchen table with a cup of hot coffee, I watched again as people with nothing but what they could carry, walked across the desert. I wondered if my life was any better than theirs. Finally, after long hours of pondering my fate, I concluded that I had my daughter, I had my health, and I was a citizen of the United States.

Over the next few months, it became obvious that my life had changed forever and that it would take a very long time for my heart to heal. Nevertheless, my child became the focus of my will to go on. She needed me. It was enough and I needed to focus on how fortunate I was compared to so many others.

Driving home from work during a stormy afternoon, Kelsy in the car seat next to mine, I turned into my gravel driveway to a sight that froze the blood in my veins. There, only feet from my car, was what seemed like dark, undulating ripples making their way toward my house. As my headlights found spaces between bursts of wind and rain, the moving mass became clearer and I began to scream. Kelsy started to cry and before long, we were both yelling at the top of our lungs. In front of us, in the tiny town of Orogrande, on a wet and stormy afternoon, I felt my worst nightmare come alive. My house stood on stilts. No one having ever bothered to enclose the space below the floors. Heading straight for it from all directions were tarantulas. Not a few, but an army of them.

Backing up, I turned the car around and didn't stop until Kelsy and I reached Grandma and Grandpa Cabbage's tiny trailer in Alamogordo.

Chapter 17

"What can we do for you, honey?" the old woman asked, her arm gently draped around my shoulders. For at least three generations she had been called Grandma Cabbage. It stuck because it was her real last name. When Grandpa Cabbage's parents immigrated to the United States from Germany, their name was Kohl. In English, the translation is either coal or cabbage. Someone in immigration had decided to have a good laugh at the expense of this young family who did not yet know the difference. Later, they were offered a chance to change their name but they decided to keep what they had been given by the authorities. It was God's will. Like their namesake, the Cabbages were decent, steady people who worked hard and tried to be good to everyone.

Grandpa had been a cowboy most of his adult life and Grandma had taught grades one through eight in a one-room schoolhouse on the Western Prairie. When their first child was born, they moved to Kalispell, Montana. Although life was hard, they got by on Grandpa's salary first as a carpenter and later as a janitor at the local high school. Retirement had given them the opportunity to move to a gentler climate in New Mexico. They had little more than the small trailer they bought when they arrived. Attached to it, Grandpa built a small living room with an even smaller storage room behind it. They were in no position to offer much help but what they did offer saved my life. They moved tools and canned goods to one side of the tiny storage area and borrowed a mattress from one of their neighbors so Kelsy and I would have a safe place to sleep.

Grandma was concerned about me. I had told her and Grandpa about Jerry leaving Kelsy and me two weeks earlier. They were nearly as overcome with grief as I was, both for me and the baby, as well as their grandson.

Today Grandma Cabbage held me for long hours in her tender arms. There was nothing to be done except cry. Tears had come at the most inconvenient of times: in the grocery store playing tinny versions of favorite songs, seeing young men playing with their children in front yards littered with toys, some of them clearly disabled. The sight of them playing with their children in spite of physical wounds tore at my mind and heart.

I had a hard time breathing and felt dizzy from lack of oxygen and the effort to make sense of the feelings that were struggling to surface.

"Grandma, I need to lie down for a few minutes. Can you watch the baby for me?"

"Of course, sweetheart. I'll put her in the highchair and give her some cereal. She can watch me make the peach cobbler we'll have tonight."

I hadn't lied. I was dizzy and had to hold on to the doorframe leading to my bedroom. Reaching toward my mattress two feet away, I fell on it, knees first. When I rolled onto my back, I could see shafts of light streaming through the small window high on the cinder block wall above Grandpa's tools and Grandma's boxes. Silence, like a warm, cozy blanket enveloped me. Then, my senses seemed to become sharper. To the soft silence surrounding me, the faint smell of sundrenched linens slapping in a gentle breeze were added along with the sight of white lace curtains drawn against a stormy sky. My mind drifted to my Oma's bedroom in East Germany where she and I had often napped together under feather quilts grown impossibly soft after decades of washings and bleachings in the sun. It was as perfect as my life had ever been and I longed to stay.

Soon, however, far too soon in my opinion, my vision began to change. My favorite room began to fade and the warm light surrounding me became brighter until it outshone everything I had ever seen. Before long, the light pulled me deeper into itself and I floated willingly into the brilliance with no end in sight. But, at some point, the light opened up to reveal an equally bright room. I could see no walls or ceiling so I suppose it could have been an outdoor space. The floor on which I stood was solid and just as bright. I had no idea how I got to this amazing place in which I found myself. I felt no fear. Even when a person dressed in white emerged from the background toward me. Not until she was near me did I see that she was a woman of indistinguishable age with long, white hair falling in waves around her shoulders and down her back.

We looked at each other some moments before we both smiled and she reached out a hand and touched my left arm. Gently, she pulled me forward, still never having said a word. Eventually I sensed that we had reached another "room." There was no discernible change that would account for my feelings. It was still a perfect temperature with the same bright illumination. The only difference was the presence of more people dressed in similar white robes to the one my guide wore. There might have been a dozen or so standing in a circle, facing me. They were different heights and had different faces but they shared the same serious and kind looks. With a slight nodding of their heads toward me, they turned back to face each other. The woman who had led me to this place looked at me intently and asked me, "What is it that you wish?"

"I want to come home." She did not laugh at me as I feared but took another moment before turning and walking to her circle. As she blended in with her companions, I became aware of conversation but could not understand a single word. There was no way of knowing how much time had passed before the being who had led me to this moment returned to my side.

"There is agreement that you may stay or return, as you please. You have earned the right to stay but there is more for you to do if you choose to return. If you stay here, you may rest until you are ready to go back. There is more for you to learn and you must learn those lessons before you can come home forever."

I woke up slowly. I couldn't leave my baby and I could not imagine having to come back. My father's words also came to mind: "Head up, shoulders back, and a smile on your face. That's right. You never know where or when the next marvelous surprise will find you."

It found me the next day in the form of a letter from the university, which I had applied to six weeks before. I was hired to be their new administrator for one of three schools available to enlisted men and women on Holloman Air Force Base.

Chapter 18

I loved almost everything about my work as administrator of a large university program. The only challenge was when I had to let one of my instructors go. He was a bright officer who taught two mathematic classes. The students hated him. Information that had been given to me by a good half of the students in his classes made it impossible for me to renew his contract for the next academic year. In my last discussion with him, he informed me that he would have me and my decision investigated.

"He may be a really fine officer but that does not necessarily make him a good instructor," I told a polite, yet firm military officer assigned to look into this situation.

"I know how you feel, but you have to realize that not being renewed for next semester's classes may have an impact on his career in the U.S. Air Force."

"I am truly sorry to hear that but I will not ignore the numerous complaints I've received from his students. He is your responsibility and they are mine."

"I can't change your mind?"

"No, but I am willing to write a statement to the effect that Captain Jones and I have tried, on several occasions, to come to an understanding about the complaints and nothing has changed over the course of this semester. I will also write a statement that my decision should not influence the evaluations of his military duties. Please remember also that I have had each and every one of my students put their concerns in writing and I have all the evaluations that are required at the end of each semester."

By the time the investigator politely shook my hand and thanked me, I was relieved to see his back. I wondered if that was the beginning of a grin when he turned away from me.

Yes, I had found my courage but my heart was still missing.

Six months after Jerry disappeared, he showed up long enough to ask me for a divorce. There was no point in refusing, so we ended our marriage in a courthouse where the presiding judge became angry with me for crying and holding on to Jerry. He thought Jerry was my new boyfriend and the reason for my divorce petition. I explained the situation and his face softened just a little.

The next year included doubling my enrollment, working late nights, and taking responsibility for a second on-base university program. The second job paid for my tuition for a master's degree in counseling. I hired a babysitter on base to take care of Kelsy while I worked or attended classes. It was convenient but I hated leaving her in someone else's care for so many hours.

With the money from my Orogrande property and a loan from my mother, I managed to make a down payment on a small, brick house on Pecan Street in Alamogordo. It had a wonderful backyard fenced by a cinder block wall. Nearly a quarter acre of lush lawn and fragrant honeysuckle bushes made it a perfect place for Kelsy to play.

On a sunny Sunday morning, she came into the bedroom I used as an office and stood next to the chair I was sitting on. I was deep in thought and scribbling study notes at the desk Grandpa Cabbage had made for me. He was, among many other things, a master carpenter and the desktop could be raised like a drafting table. Pulling at my blouse, Kelsy looked beseechingly at my distracted face.

"Please, Mommy, can we go to the park?"

I pulled my thoughts away from the notes I was working on and looked into the angelic face that looked so much like her father's and I felt a familiar twist in my heart. All her friends lived on Holloman Base and she rarely had a chance to see them when we were home. The park took less than five minutes to get to and we both needed some time together.

"Yes, sweetheart, let's go play."

She squealed as she danced out of my office and was just starting to turn into the hall when the doorbell rang. Both of us froze in our tracks. We seldom expected anyone and there were no plans for visitors today. Kelsy reached the door before me but I pushed her back while I unlocked and opened it. It was Jerry. Kelsy screamed and pushed past me to fling herself into her father's arms. I stood back as they hugged and kissed.

Looking past our little girl's shoulder, Jerry looked at me and said, "Can I come in? I didn't have a chance to let you know that I'm in town but I really would like to talk to you."

The park forgotten, we walked into the living room and Jerry sat on the floor with Kelsy in his lap. I sat in the only chair, a rocker, I had bought when Kelsy was born.

"I've been living an hours' drive from here in Roswell."

My heart skipped a beat.

"How long have you been there?"

"About eight months."

"Why haven't you called or come by?"

"I didn't want to face you. Besides, I needed time to do some thinking."

"What is it you want to talk about now?"

"Karin, I want to get married again." My heart skipped a beat and I had to lower my head so Jerry wouldn't see the joy in my face.

"Her name is Connie and I know I haven't paid any child support but when Connie and I get married we'll both have jobs and I can afford to catch up with what I owe you. She's a bartender at the hotel in town and makes good money and I'll work making furniture at her brother's shop."

"So you came here today to tell me that you are getting married again?"

"Well, no. I mean yes, that's a part of it. But the real reason I need to talk to you is to ask if you'd let Kelsy be a part of the wedding. Connie has two small boys and we thought the kids could get to know each other. We have rabbit hutches in the back and chicken coops and cats and dogs. Kelsy would have a great time."

"How long do you want her?"

"A week, starting tomorrow. The wedding is next Saturday so there will be a few days for me to spend with my daughter and for her to get to know her other family."

I had no idea what to feel. My face had flushed when he said he wanted to get married again and now I felt myself pale as blood drained from my head into my toes. He looked so happy, so full of life and hope for the future. He looked younger than when he left and I felt ancient. There was my answer, I felt old. I also felt weak and hollow. My heart had broken into a million shards and I had no idea how to find those pieces again much less put them together.

My blessings were a good job and a roof over our heads. But, what I could not give my daughter was her father and a family.

"Okay. I'll pack some of her things and have her ready for you tomorrow. But, you have to let her call me every day so I can make sure she is happy."

"That's no problem. Oh, and by the way, do you still have the shirt you made me when we got to Orogrande? I don't have anything nice to wear to my wedding."

Numb, I told him I would have it, and Kelsy, and the things she would need for a week ready for him when he picked her up.

Part VII

Moving On

Chapter 19

I had learned how to bear loss and I had learned how to be courageous. What I had not yet learned was how to make choices other than by default. I reacted to someone else's choices and survived. It was time to make decisions based on my own visions for my life.

But what was it that I wanted? It wasn't necessarily an easy life. For sure, I wanted a meaningful life. So, what was meaningful for me? Victor Frankl, famous psychologist and survivor of the horrors of Auschwitz, once said, "To choose one's attitude is the last of the freedoms." So, first I had to choose an attitude toward life in general and mine in particular. I made a list of all the things that had ever been said or done to me that I did not think were fair. It was a relatively long list. It started with my mother taking me from my home and family. It ended with Jerry leaving our little girl and me in the middle of a desert. In both cases, there was no warning. Another person came to mind as I reviewed my past. Grandpa Professor. I had felt helpless and I had felt fear.

What was my attitude toward these events and people? I loved them and wanted to make them happy and proud of me. I wanted to lose the pain that thoughts of them bubbled up from my core. At that moment, I realized that only I had the option to continue the pain or realize that I could forgive them. They were simply living out their own realities and choices. And, if I could not wholly change my attitude permanently, I could start practicing.

Then I made a longer list of all the wonderful things I had experienced and the extraordinary people that had been or were still in my life. In a single flash of insight, I became aware of how fortunate I was to have such a rich life of both lessons and joy. So what did I want?

I wanted a second chance at love. Was there anyone who could capture my heart the way Jerry had? My soul yearned for intimacy but my ego wanted it on its own terms. That had to change.

I wanted to be a part of a loving family of my own with Kelsy at the center, and perhaps, siblings for her. Because I knew that the inner always creates the outer, it meant I needed to grow in mindfulness.

I wanted to earn a Ph.D. That meant I had to move to a larger city. I still loved the relative seclusion of a small town in New Mexico but a change would be welcome. If I was going to change my life, it made sense to change completely. Alaska came to mind.

Most of all, I wanted to be a good person. Not a Nazi like some had labeled me, not a "bad seed" as Grandpa Professor had called me, and not arrogant or aloof, a persona stemming from my shyness.

That's a lot of wanting but I thought I was up to making the changes that would move me forward in the direction I longed my life to take.

"Mommy, can I take this?" Kelsy was three years old now and understood that we were going to leave our house and move somewhere far away. She also knew that she would not be able to see her daddy or her new family as much. I had reassured her that Jerry would come to visit her as much as he could and that all of her new family would always love her. Still, she cried and I ached for her.

"Of course you can. That's your favorite bear. Let's find a

big box from the stack in the garage so you can take all your animal friends. We don't want to leave anyone behind."

The ruffles on Kelsy's little dress rippled to the rhythm of her running feet. She beat me to the garage and started to pick boxes she liked and put them in a separate pile next to her. We sorted through what would be best for the different things we had to pack and when she was satisfied, she made several trips with empty boxes to her bedroom.

While Kelsy busied herself with her own packing, I decided what I could give away and what I needed to keep in order to start a new life. Once again, I reviewed my list of things to do. I had sold the house and would have to be moved out within the week. The long rental truck would be available in four days. Some of my students had offered to help me load up. I had hired replacements for my jobs at the air base. My bills were caught up and most of my goodbyes were said. The only thing that remained, and the hardest, was saying goodbye to Grandma and Grandpa Cabbage. Five days later, I pulled up to the curb in front of the trailer park where my dearest living grandparents lived their simple lives.

When Kelsy and I neared the old Silverstream, we could see the two with their arms wrapped around each other's shoulders and waving with their free hands. They couldn't move and we could not run fast enough to join in the embrace. Hugging and crying, no words were spoken. There was no need for words. Eventually, Kelsy and I separated ourselves from two of the dearest people I knew and made our way back to the truck. When we were strapped in, I put the giant vehicle into gear and started driving. It was the first time I had chosen to leave people who loved me and didn't want to see me go.

Chapter 20

The truck wasn't easy to drive but it wasn't hard either. I had left shortly after noon and that meant I would be driving through the night in order to get to Studio City in California without an overnight stay somewhere. I wanted to say goodbye to my mother and Knut before settling in Alaska. It was when I was driving through a long valley sometime around one in the morning that I remembered taking this road in the opposite direction toward Colorado a couple of years before Kelsy was born. I had been driving my red VW Bug in the middle of the night near Four Corners, the place where Colorado, New Mexico, Arizona, and Utah meet. A lot of the road I was on went through Navajo country and many people had warned me for years about the dangers of that stretch of road. I was driving over the speed limit by about ten miles per hour and climbing a steep slope that ended in a long curve to the left. I had driven this stretch of road at least a dozen times without any incidents. The momentum I had built up prior to the incline kept my red "bug" going at a good clip when the dark night gave me a glimpse of an even blacker shape on the road ahead. There was no time to stop or even slow down so I could do little more than stare as the black shape came closer and my front tires fit neatly on the hoofs, then legs, and finally, the black body of the sheep that had been laid in my path. Rather than stopping me or even slowing me down, the sheep acted like a springboard that sent my car into the void, nose first so that I lost sight of the road and anything else except dark sky. I remembered that one of the Indian strategies was to claim that a tourist had run over a prime sheep and therefore owed the cost of the sheep as well as the value of any sheep the dead one might have produced in its lifetime, and their collective value. I landed on the road just as it was starting its curve and had only a moment to look into the rearview mirror to see two men on the road next to the sheep, staring in my direction.

The rest of this drive was uneventful. There was still beautiful countryside to get through, but because it was dark, I only saw the highway stretch out in front of me. I had plenty of time to think. My little Kelsy was now four years old and sleeping on the passenger seat next to me. Seatbelts were not required, and in fact, most cars didn't have them. Her head was scrunched against my thigh and the rest of her body stretched under a mound of blankets.

My thoughts traced a line of events from the day I met Jerry to the day he walked out on us. My life had changed when we met and it had changed even more when he left. In the first part, I had learned to love and trust again. Then I had remembered how to lose and survive loneliness. Now I had a child to love and take care of and enough experience to know I *could* take care of us. It was progress, if you didn't consider how desperately I longed for the warmth of family.

"Why then do I want to visit my mother in L.A. on the way to a new start?" I asked myself. There was no warmth there. At least not often. But, she had been my only family for so long that I accepted her inability to genuinely feel love and accepted her disingenuous affection as something better than nothing. And, if I'm to be honest, a part of me still wanted her show of affection to be real. My mind continued to meander on these detours as well as toward the future I envisioned in Alaska, until I came to the outskirts of Los Angeles. Lights, noise, and smog assaulted my senses from Bakersfield onwards. By the time I got to Studio City and parked my long truck across the street from my mother's house, it was midmorning. Kelsy was hungry and I desperately needed sleep.

"Hi, Mom."

"My children, my children," she squealed. She held out her arms and before I could embrace her, she bent down and picked up Kelsy still shouting in a singsong voice that we were her children. Kelsy started to cry and I followed them both into the house. When my mother turned to me and held out her free arm to me, I hugged her, glad to be in her arms again. How was it that I never lost hope that my mother's exuberance and delight to see me would last. Experience told me that I was crazy to think our relationship could ever change. But, here was the truth, I didn't have another mother and no relatives to call family. I needed her in whatever way she was available to me.

Knut came into the entry hall where we were still standing and smiled his welcome. He had never had children of his own so he gently pulled on Kelsy's hand and said, "Hi." It was enough to distract her and she stopped crying. She wiggled out of my mother's grasp and immediately headed toward the smell of delicious food. Knut had cooked his famous goulash for us. It reminded me that I was hungry, too.

"We'll only be here three or four days," I told my mother. "There's a teaching job waiting for me in Fairbanks and I need time to get there and find a place to live and babysitter for Kelsy. I'll manage but we have to leave by the end of the week."

"But I don't want you to go so soon. You just got here and there's plenty of room. Besides, you know how hard it is to live with Knut."

"Mom, even if I stayed another few days, it would not help your relationship. That's something you have to do by yourself. Besides, this is a wonderful opportunity for me."

"What about what I want? Well, never mind. I can see how much I mean to you."

The next day Kelsy was running a high fever. The usual over-the-counter medications didn't seem to help much and I spent that night awake holding and comforting her as much as I could. It was no good. She woke the next morning even more feverish and all I could get her to swallow was a bit of apple juice diluted with water. I had no health insurance for us being between jobs, but there was no choice. I bundled her up, because even in the heat of a Southern California summer, she was shaking with cold.

The wait in the emergency room was unpleasant and long. Kelsy had stopped whimpering and lay limp in my arms. By the time we were called in to one of the examination rooms my little girl was burning with fever and I was panicked. The doctor, a young man in a white coat at least two sizes too big for him, walked in with a serious look on his face.

He looked at Kelsy in my arms shaking from fever and cold.

"Put her on the table, chest up."

The paper on which I placed her crinkled as I put her down and she whimpered weakly. The doctor gently took her hand and softly asked her, "Can you tell me what's hurting? All Kelsy could do was look at him with blurry, red eyes and roll her head away from him.

"Well then, let's see if we can figure this out and make you feel better."

The result was severe infections in both ears that would require drainage and implanting tubes in both ear canals. Then, if everything went well, medication to insure that infections would not set in again. In other words, hospitalization. I did as the doctor advised and Kelsy received the treatment she needed.

Unfortunately, the infections returned repeatedly. There was no permanent solution and no moving to Alaska.

When I called my intended employers in Fairbanks, I also

started my job search in L.A. I needed money desperately to pay for medical care and to rebuild life in our unexpected new location. Mother was anxious to have her privacy again and asked pointed questions about when I would find a place to live.

"Have you found work yet? You know Kelsy needs a permanent home."

These were two of the points she made almost daily. I took a temporary job as a receptionist in a dental office until something better came along. It helped with expenses but was in no way sufficient to become independent.

Salvation came in the way of a phone call from UCLA where I had put in an application. They were looking for a full-time employee in the College of Letters and Science counseling office. The work was a perfect fit for my qualifications and the fact that I had been a student there was an advantage. I had just enough time to find an apartment and move before my new job started. Mother refused to care for Kelsy and told me that since I chose to have the child, she was my responsibility. Luckily, I found a babysitter near our complex so that life had an element of normalcy and hope again. The only problem was that I was still desperately lonely.

Chapter 21

Loneliness dogged my every step. There was not one day when I did not spend some time dreaming about having a loving partner and father for Kelsy. My dream of living in Alaska stayed with me as well. Somehow, though, I could never save enough money to make that a reality.

Then there was the depression. Most evenings now I opened a bottle of wine after Kelsy was in bed and sleeping. Tonight, a glass of wine, a roaring fire and winter winds howling outside the door define this frosty night. Like a stranger to myself, I watched in growing alarm as the clutter of thoughts and feelings that controlled me for so many years, threatened to unravel the threads of my sanity. A lifetime of countless tiny decisions paved the path toward this moment. Tonight, whispering voices speak inside my head. Or is it the wine releasing its toxins? But the blurring of sharp edges around my thoughts brings no ease, merely a dulling of pain. Within a fold of my heart hides a longing for something lost. I have only one real hope. To start remembering what I have worked so hard to forget and to rediscover the source of strength that made survival possible in my past and for the women who came before me. I feel bound by history and by a responsibility to create a viable future. Also, to help anyone else in my life who hopes for possibilities and choice. Possibilities of self-discovery and growth. Possibilities of personal freedom and strength.

The immediate concern, then, is lifting thick layers of amnesia binding forgotten dimensions of childhood and youthful experiences. Not only was secrecy an integral part of my early life to hide certain abuses, but it was used by my elders to add meaning and honor to lives that had little of either. Hidden memories and lost senses, which once defined the child and young adult that I used to be were emerging from the confusion shaping my life today. It was a relief to know that the layers of forgetting which shrouded my adult life served the rather essential purpose of survival. It was not a fluke that my mind chose to reject certain information in its attempt to adjust to experiences and demands it was ill equipped to integrate. It was much easier to remember the love that had compelled my father to ride the train into our town and hide behind the hedge, which had once been the scene of my own violation in order to watch me play for a few hours.

I had no idea when my parents were divorced. The East German government, controlled by Russia, assigned my father to another town to work and he had never lived with us that I could remember. But, his absences were the result of a court order. He'd been forbidden any contact with me by judges who ruled the conditions of my parents' legal separation. His act of disobedience meant love to me.

It was heartwarming to recall the living room scene a year before my mother and I escaped to West Germany when my father once more declared his love for my mother.

"Ella, you know I love you. From the first time I laid eyes on you in the school gym when you were only fourteen years old, I've known that we were meant to be together. I may have made some mistakes in the past but you have to admit that a divorce isn't right for any of us, especially our little Karin."

I sat on his knee crying and hoping that she would accept his apologies. How could I have known as I sat on my dad's knee and wept with him that my mother had already begun preparations for their divorce and our escape to America.

So many more things from a clouded past needed my review, but at that moment, my numb legs and aching back demanded relief. At three o'clock in the morning, I had to get some sleep. Tired, but somehow lighter, my body creaked into mobility and I gathered my notes into a neat pile beside my chair. I had never been able to dismiss my compulsive neatness and only when the empty wine glass was rinsed and set aside next to the sink was I able to take myself to bed.

Exhaustion claimed my mind after a brief moment of pleasure remembering that the next day I was invited to a party. It had been almost three years since I'd participated in any social event with the exception of work-related lunches. In fact, I was more excited than I thought I would be. Even more surprising was the sense of tension I felt. In one moment, I wanted to abandon myself to a good time with good people. The next moment I knew that nothing would feel safer than my own company and the warmth of my lonely bed.

Chapter 22

The party had been nice enough with Eleanor and I drinking and giggling like the teenagers we would never be again.

Leni, who didn't like being called Eleanor, was my colleague and best friend at work. We were the odd couple in our counseling unit in UCLA. We talked about being women in a man's world. We talked about raising our children without fathers. We even discussed the challenges of Jewish and German history. "Such a nice German girl you are."

Tonight we were at the party together in Temple Valley Beth Shalom on Ventura Boulevard in Encino. We each nursed a glass of wine strategically sitting so we faced the crowded dance floor. We had both declined a handful of men seeking dance partners.

We had seen a few nice young men hunting for a night's pleasure with equally nice young women hunting for a lifetime commitment. I didn't feel nice and I wasn't young. At thirty, I was too old to be cute and too young to know that married bliss was a fantasy. Somehow, against all the odds, I was sure that love would still find me, and beating the odds would make it that much sweeter.

When I thought about the milestones in my life that had brought me to this place and time I could not help but think of Herr Professor. It was that grandfather, who, while abusing me, taught me his turn-of-the-century, old world morality. I had never quite outgrown it and it was the standard against which I railed, yet which I desperately sought to personify. So, on this particular night, I would once again pit my rebellious nature against the standard of good behavior I had been taught.

There were more people at the party than I could count. Bodies spilled into every room. Leni left early and I was content to sit at one of the small tables listening to older women gossip about the very young who were playing the eternal mating game with ribbons in their hair, lowered lashes, and outbursts of giggles. And older men, looking rheumatic and bored, who, in spite of sagging vigor, would squeeze a twinkle out of their eyes and accidentally rub an arthritic knee against a fleshy, young thigh. I sat smiling vacantly at the antics around my table. I had primped a full two hours in preparation for this event and I looked good. I would look even better once I finished paying for the contact lenses on layaway until next month. I was embarrassed about the outdated glasses I repeatedly removed whenever a man passed close enough to take a good look. This did not happen often with the older men and women at my table presenting a rather formidable barrier to most casual advances.

Leni had decided to leave after finishing her glass of wine but I was still nursing mine, reluctant to waste a drop. I knew it was time to leave when a not-so-young man leaned over my shoulder and slurred something about wanting to dance with me. It was uncertain whether he could safely stand up on his own, much less dance. Making some excuses, I unhooked my purse from the back of my chair and hurried out the door.

Behind the wheel of my car, windows down, I sat with eyes fixed on nothing, hands limp on my lap. A sporadic, hot breeze rippled my hair and dried the tears spilling from my eyes. My mind asked how I could possibly be the soft-spoken essence of Victorian femininity. How could I tame the urgings of my body and beat my inquisitive mind into submission? Yet, I retained the hope that I would someday transform my rebellious flesh and perverse mind into the model of decorum I required of myself. Self-worth and respectability. I craved them both. In angry frustration I beat my fists onto the steering wheel in time to the sobs I could no longer hold back, until finally, my anger spent, I lowered my head to my hands still clutching the top of the wheel. Lonely, desperately lonely. Angry, too. Angry that I could not let go of the hope of having someone to love me someday.

Vaguely aware of people passing my car and looking at me with concern or amusement, I fumbled for my key on the seat next to mine and shakily inserted it into the ignition.

Chapter 23

It was Friday evening and I was driving home after a meeting that ran over at work. Kelsy was at a friend's house spending the night with a girl from her gym class. Because there was no rush, I stopped for dinner at an outdoor eatery in Westwood before driving over Coldwater Canyon to my apartment in Encino.

East on Ventura Boulevard along the glittering lights of shops for the wealthy and clubs for the teeming hordes of perfumed men and women dressed to attract and repel, couples held hands and walked or sat at bistro tables. Endless rows of dazzling colors, swirling costumes and sleek automobiles. Right on Van Nuys Boulevard. Only three more blocks and I would be able to see the back of my second-story apartment. An old, two-bedroom affair so hot you couldn't touch the walls in summer. The landlady had promised a swamp cooler two years ago but never delivered. Every time I reminded her, she threatened to raise the rent. I couldn't afford that so I had stopped asking.

When I unlocked the door the silence was even more oppressive than the heat. The lights from neighboring apartments were enough to find my way to the bedroom. Shorts and a t-shirt replaced my dress and sandals slipped more easily ono my swollen feet than the heels I was wearing. As neighbors turned off their lights and went to bed, a gloom enveloped me the likes of which I had never experienced. I could hardly breathe.

My mind went blank and I could do nothing more than stand in the middle of my dark kitchen, a glass of water poised half way to my mouth. Immobile, I tried to find thoughts that made sense. I knew they lingered somewhere but I could not find them. The only thoughts that penetrated my consciousness were registering my immobility. I had to move. But where and how?

Slowly, my legs jerked of their own accord and like a puppet's on faulty strings, I felt myself move down stairs and onto a sidewalk I had taken little notice of. Usually, I drove to my apartment and parked in a space designated for my use at the back of the building. Tonight my legs carried me down the street in front of my home and across traffic lanes empty at this hour. The farther I walked the less streetlights lit the night.

Eventually, I came to a hedge overgrown with vines and dead streamers of foliage. There was enough moonlight to help me see my way through the undergrowth and into roughly two acres of magical garden. Natural rock formations had become perfect ledges like benches waiting just for me. I sat down and looked at the expanse of rich grass bordered on all sides by towering trees separating this oasis from the rest of the world. A soft mist lay around me and softened shadowy trees on the far side of the lawn. Moonshine lit particles of airborne water so that it seemed to me that the air was filled with diamonds. Nothing could have prepared me for the sheer beauty of this moment and this place.

I began to breathe deeply and with my hands explored the grass and rocky shelf on which I sat. A thought penetrated my consciousness. In that moment of profound silence and natural beauty, I realized that I was not separate from any of the life around me. The "self" I had always thought as separate and individual was as much a part of the world as my breath was a part of me. The sorrow I felt did not extend beyond me but was a unique part of my own experience of life. As such, it was mine to hold onto or mine to release. The feelings of abandonment and being unlovable had no more power over me than I chose to give them. They had become a part of my experience and identity because they were once true for me and I had clung to them and mistaken them for my true self.

The tears came, at first like a rainstorm breaking from thundering sobs. For longer than I could tell, wrenching pain and tears tore at me like talons ripping apart the spoils of a kill.

Slowly, as my body emptied itself of attachment to the feelings of the past and the demands I made of myself for a future I had dreamed of for as long as I could remember, I saw that I clung to my pain like a dear friend. The normalcy I had fought so hard to achieve was simply another illusion. It was an attempt to be like I imagined "others" were and thereby a betrayal of myself. I moaned as I realized my only task was to be true to who I was and had always been. Life would bring me the opportunities that I was ready to experience. With a mind free of the shackles of my own judgments, I could let my heart free to feel all it was capable of feeling.

The moon was still high and bright in the night sky when I stepped into my hot apartment again. I thought about people huddled in cold misery wishing for just a small bit of the warmth I felt. A slight, cool breeze beckoned me from the open window in my bedroom and led me to that room and the bed that felt softer than I remembered.

Chapter 24

It was another late evening in my office at Antelope Valley University. The class I had finished teaching just minutes before was about communication and perception. My students' papers lay scattered across my desk in piles according to the essay question each student chose to answer. There were five possibilities and I was eager to see what they had to say. But it was nearly nine in the evening and the music concert in the building across the quad had just ended. Like the people streaming out of the concert hall, I was ready to leave but decided to let most of the people leave before I joined the mob and cars at the only exit remaining open at this hour.

A door slammed in the hall and lights that had been turned off sprang to life. Laughing voices preceded the couple that entered the bank of counseling offices and stopped at the counter where groups of students usually gathered. My office and desk faced the counter and I saw one of my colleagues dressed in her finest concert gown enter the common space followed by a tall man dressed in a black tuxedo. His bowtie was white, unlike most of the men in the United States who wear black.

Colleen waved to me as she steered her date around the counter and into my office. Still draped across his right arm while he stood ramrod straight, they squeezed through my door side by side. I invited them to sit in the two "student" chairs across from my desk.

"This is Karl, my cousin from Sweden. You remember him." Indeed I did. Several months prior, Colleen had asked me to review Karl's educational and professional documentation and help him put together a résumé in the hopes of obtaining work in California. By then he had been divorced almost two years and was considering a move to the States. I had been happy to assist and had been impressed with the qualifications this man had sent me.

Colleen sat bubbling with excitement while her cousin sat quietly in the chair next to hers. "He's going to stay with me for the next two weeks while he interviews for jobs here in Southern California."

"That brings me to something I want to say to you." Almost formally, Karl stood up and reached in his left pocket to withdraw a small package before offering his right hand in my direction. In a heavily accented, solemn tone he said, "I want to thank you for the help you have given to me. It is so very much appreciated." With that, he extended the package in my direction and sat back down.

"Thank you." As I unwrapped the ribbon and opened the box, a sigh escaped my lips and my vision began to blur. In the box lay a glass globe reminiscent of the moonlit fog I had once seen during a midnight confrontation with past suffering. But, instead of a moon, the glass globe's fog was penetrated by a clear blue triangle speckled with golden flecks.

"I never expected anything in return for what I gladly did for you. The beauty of your gift leaves me breathless and I don't know what to say."

"I am happy you like it."

As I held out the gift box to Colleen, I asked, "Have you seen this?"

She looked across my desk and giggled before returning her smile to Karl. "He has really good taste. We have to leave now because I want to introduce him to more of my friends. Some of us are meeting at Far West for drinks."

All three of us rose and I said "thank you" one more time before Colleen and her cousin exited; I gathered my things before locking up and turning out the lights.

Chapter 25

A few months later in the early fall of 1998, Colleen called on a Friday evening to ask if I could pick up her cousin from Sweden at LAX later that same evening. I had no plans so I told her I would pick Karl up from the international terminal and drop him off at her house.

His arrival was on time and I waited at the top of the ramp hoping he would recognize me. I need not have worried. When he came up the ramp dragging a battered old suitcase, he glanced to the top of the ramp where I was waiting for him. His smile left no doubt that he recognized me and that he was glad to see me there.

A brief greeting and a handshake "hello" were sufficient to reestablish the connection we had made on his previous visit.

When we got into my car and settled comfortably into our seats, he told me that Colleen had texted him that I would be able to pick him up and hoped he would not mind that she was not able to come herself.

"I know that Colleen is afraid to drive on freeways so I am very glad you are willing to do this for me."

"This is not a problem and I'm glad to help."

"You don't know how much I appreciate how much you've done for me. I don't know how to thank you enough."

"Like I said, I'm glad to help and if there is anything else I can do, please let me know."

We were on the 405 Freeway going north toward Palmdale and Lancaster when Karl turned to me and said, "Actually, I would very much like to visit UCLA and I know that you work there. Is there any chance that you can take me along one day and I can look around the campus while you work?"

"That's easy. I can pick you up Monday morning and we can drive together. Between seeing students I can show you around. It's an interesting place and I think you will enjoy whatever lectures you want to attend or museums you want to visit. The campus has endless possibilities for exploration and we can have lunch at the faculty club. It's a short walk from my office in Murphy Hall."

The day couldn't have been more perfect. The weather was what California is famous for...warm and sunny. The blue sky was free of smog and a slight breeze fanned palms and wispy shrubs. While I worked, Karl had found his way from one end of the campus to the other, a little like exploring a small city. Lunch was lovely on the outside terrace of the faculty club with tables scattered around ancient trees and colorful bougainvillea.

Going north again on the 405 turned out to be impossible. There had been an accident where the 405 and Ventura Freeways meet and traffic was stopped in all directions. The wait was estimated to be at least two hours.

"If you would like to go up the coast instead of waiting in traffic, I can take you over Mulholland Drive and down the west side of the Santa Monica mountains to Pacific Coast Highway."

His smile was enough even before he said he would love to do just that.

North through Malibu and up toward Ventura, we drove in

the warm breeze off the Pacific Ocean. I suggested we stop at my favorite beach, Leo Carillo, and Karl enthusiastically agreed.

Because it was a weekday, few people enjoyed the beauty and solitude of the rocks and sand at this particularly beautiful spot along the coast. Karl and I waded in the water and finally sat on a large rock dangling our legs in the ocean and looking west across the watery horizon.

We shared a few stories of our past and a few dreams for the future. His, of course included immigrating to the United States and mine included a five-week trip to China starting in just a week. It was hard to leave but we finally made our way back to the car and home. We arrived at our destination no later than if we would have chosen to drive on the freeway and felt the detour had been a much better choice.

Later that night, amidst many apologies, Karl called me and asked if I could pick him up and if he could spend the night in my guest room. Colleen was enraged that we had spent time on the beach and wanted him out of her house and sight. He assured me that he would rent a car the following day and get a hotel room for the remainder of his stay for his job interviews.

"Of course. I'll be right there. I have a room for my granddaughter and another for my grandson. You can take your pick."

The following day I asked Karl to stay at my house until I returned from work and we could talk. When I came home, we had a chance to discuss options. Karl had several interviews scheduled for the following weeks. I had an empty house with a pool and plants that needed attention.

"How about staying in this house while I'm gone? You can take care of the place and use my car to get to your interviews and whatever else you need."

We agreed that was the very best solution for both our needs.

I had a lot to think about those next weeks in China. I loved being immersed in a culture I knew only from books. There were over a dozen of us faculty members and our "guide" was a professor who had been born and raised in China. He took us to places usually off the beaten path and I loved every moment of discovery. What I thought about most nights though was my growing attachment to Karl. In temples and ruins, I could imagine his reactions to what I was experiencing. There was no doubt that it mattered to me what he thought of me but there had never been a word of affection between us or hint of passion. A gentleman to his core, Karl never presumed anything nor had he ever invaded my privacy.

That left me with only my own feelings to guide me. But what exactly were those? I had spent so long thinking that my desire for love would go unmet that I had stopped looking or even hoping for it. It was a relief not to wait for the phone to ring and my mind had filled the spaces of my soul that were left open by my heart. But these were only thoughts and had little value in knowing my feelings. My soul yearned for intimacy but my ego wanted it on its own terms. And because the inner always creates the outer, I had created a life of lonely self sufficiency. Fear of being hurt had bound me to limitations.

And the truth is that self-discovery is necessary for growth. I could not change anyone else in order to feel safe, but I could dare to move beyond the place where my feelings of fear had made me stuck. It was up to me to embrace the changes that might be required because at the heart of stagnation is an endless repetition of unwanted outcomes.

Once again, life had given me an opportunity to feel, even love, without attachment and expectations. It is attachments, from which we expect certain outcomes, that when they fail to manifest, cut like sharp knives and make us bleed.

When my plane landed at LAX after a very long flight from Taiwan, my heart beat wildly. Karl would be there to pick me up. It seemed like an endless trek from the cockpit and exit door and down the long walkway connecting the plane to the terminal. Everyone seemed to shuffle along burdened by too much oversized luggage and swarms of cranky children.

Behind the crowd of waiting families and friends, Karl waited for me. His smile matched mine and I knew that I had come home and back to myself.

Note to Reader

There is great power in recognizing that no one has the ability to change someone else. There is no way to love enough, discipline enough, beg enough or suffer enough to change the course someone has chosen for themselves. The power in recognizing that truth is the power that sets us free. Truly and utterly free.

In the morning, sunshine still crisp,

a breeze combs my hair.

Past and present quiver with each beat of my heart

and I remember words hidden in a recess of my mind.

Fear wraps itself around the crevices of thoughts barely formed.

Still, hope ignites tomorrow.

www.ingramcontent.com/pod-product-compliance
Lightning Source LLC
Chambersburg PA
CBHW061445040426
42450CB00007B/1220